Our Broken Family Court System

Lenore E.A. Walker, Ed.D., A.B.P.P.

Dorothy M. Cummings, L.C.S.W.

Nicholas A. Cummings, Ph.D., Sc.D.

Editors

IP

ITHACA PRESS

NEW YORK

Ithaca Press
3 Kimberly Drive, Suite B
Dryden, New York 13053 USA
www.IthacaPress.com

Copyright © 2012

Our Broken Family Court System

Dr. Nicholas Cummings

| Cover Design | Gary Hoffman |
| Book Design | Gary Hoffman |

Manufactured in the United States of America

9 8 7 6 5 4 3 2 1

Library of Congress Cataloging-in-Data Available

First Edition

Printed in the United States of America

ISBN 978-0-9839121-6-3

www.PrescientBooks.com
www.DrNicholasCummings.com

This book is based on the provocative and prescient
presentations by renown national authorities at the
"Our Broken Family Court" Conference held
March 16 and 17, 2012 in Phoenix, Arizona

Cosponsored by the Nicholas & Dorothy Cummings Foundation
and the National Alliance of Professional Psychology Providers

Conference Faculty and Presenters

Robert Adler, J.D.

Mr. Adler is a partner at Adler & Kleinman Law, a New Jersey firm that focuses on Family Law in cases of child abuse and domestic violence. Formerly a criminal defense attorney for many years, he has used the criminal law to hold abusers responsible for violent behavior. He is also Vice President of the Center for the Protection of Children.

G. Andrew H. Benjamin, J.D., Ph.D., A.B.P.P.

Author of *Family Evaluation in Custody Evaluation*, Dr. Benjamin is the Director of the Custody Evaluation Center at the University of Washington in Seattle. He is both a lawyer and a family psychologist and uses his training in both areas to provide comprehensive evaluations of access to children. He is also in the independent practice of psychology and law, and is on the American Board of Psychology's American Academy of Couples and Family Psychology.

John Caccavale, Ph.D., M.S.C.P.

Dr. Caccavale is a neuropsychologist and the Executive Director of the National Alliance of Professional Psychology Providers (NAPPP), the conference's cosponsor. He is also a diplomate of the American Board of Medical Psychology. Dr. Caccavale is a longtime advocate for the advancement of clinical and medical psychology and its inclusion into primary behavioral healthcare. Over the years he has published numerous articles and book reviews, but in recent years he has confined his writing to the current issues facing the profession. Dr. Caccavale is a strong advocate for doctoral level psychology, and although he is trained as a psychopharmacologist, he advocates for psychotherapy as a first line treatment for behavioral disorders.

Dr. Caccavale serves on the Board of Medical Psychology, the National Institute of Behavioral Health Quality, The American Board of Behavioral Health Practice, and is the Chair of the Behavioral Health Committee of Orange County (California) Medical Reserve Corps. He is the 2011 recipient of the Cummings *PSYCHE* Award, with its $50,000 prize, psychology's highest award.

Janet L. Cummings, Psy.D.

An accomplished psychologist and psychotherapist, Dr. Cummings is the author of over two dozen journal articles and book chapters, and she has co-authored or co-edited 9 books with her father, Dr. Nicholas Cummings. She serves as President of the Conference's cosponsor, the Nicholas & Dorothy Cummings Foundation, a post she has held since its inception.

At the present time she is Founder's Adjunct Professor in the Nicholas A. Cummings Doctor of Behavioral Health Program, Arizona State University. She is also Adjunct Professor at both the University of Nevada, Reno and the Forrest Institute of Professional Psychology in Springfield, MO. In conjunction with her father she has conducted numerous one and two week training courses in the Biodyne Model, one in London for the National Health Service. She is a survivor of the family court system.

Dorothy M. Cummings, L.C.S.W.

As a social worker, Dorothy Cummings has worked in a variety of settings, ranging from public assistance to school social work. She is a Charter Member of the National Association of Social Work, dating back to its pre-founding in 1955. From their inception, she has served on the Boards as Secretary/Treasurer of both the Nicholas & Dorothy Cummings Foundation (cosponsor of this conference) and the Cummings Foundation for Behavioral Health. A surviving grandmother of the family court system, she was co-organizer of this conference with Dr. Walker.

Nicholas A. Cummings, Ph.D., Sc.D.

Dr. Cummings is a visionary and a psychologist, who for half a century was not only able to foresee the future of professional psychology, he helped create it. Along the way he has innovated steps to enhance the profession. He has authored or edited 49 books. His pioneering "intermittent, focused psychotherapy throughout the life cycle" (also known as the Biodyne Model, two Greek words meaning "life change") is the way most psychologists practice today. He was active with the Dirty Dozen for 30 years, founded the professional school movement through the four campuses of the California School of Professional Psychology, created the only psychology-driven national healthcare company which grew in all 50 states to 25 million covered lives in which psychiatric/medical directors reported to psychologists, and a host of other innovations too numerous to mention.

He served as President of the American Psychological Association, has six honorary doctorates, and holds every honor the profession can bestow, including the APF Gold Medal. In 2008, he designed, and with Arizona State University, launched the state-of-the-art Doctor of Behavioral Health Program which bears his name. At the present time he is Distinguished Founding Professor at Arizona State University; Distinguished Professor of Psychology, University of Nevada, Reno; and active president of the Cummings Foundation for Behavioral Health, as well as chair of the Board of the Nicholas & Dorothy Cummings Foundation.

Leslie Drozd, Ph.D.

Dr. Drozd is a psychologist, author, and an editor of an international journal, the *Journal of Child Custody*. Most importantly, she has been involved in training family court judges for the past 10 years, and helping to educate all who work in the Family Courts. She currently has an independent practice as well as providing expert testimony in Family Court. She has conducted child custody evaluations for over 20 years, as well post-divorce work with families including reunification therapy when the child has rejected a parent.

She has been a speaker on issues of alleged abuse, neglect, and endangerment, and she helped create the Model Standards for Conducting Child Custody Evaluations for the Association of Family and Conciliation Courts.

Hon. Marjory D. Fields, J.D.

Judge Fields is the author of *Diversion Is Dangerous, Getting Beyond What Did She Do to Provoke Him?* She was Family and Superior Court Judge in New York City from 1986 to 2002 and Supervising Judge of the Family Court in Bronx, NY for eight years. Prior to being appointed to the bench, Judge Fields was an attorney in a family law practice in federally funded legal services for the poor for 15 years. Judge Fields participated in the first law suit against New York City Courts for failure to provide adequate services and protect battered women over 30 years ago. She continues to write and advocate for protection for domestic violence victims.

Ricky Greenwald, Psy.D.

Dr. Greenwald is an Affiliate Professor at the SUNY University at Buffalo, and was previously Assistant Clinical Professor and Director of Training for the child trauma program at Mount Sinai School of Medicine (NYC), Department of Psychiatry. He has also served as Senior Psychologist with the Mokihana Project (Kauai, HI), a project providing child/family mental health services via the public school system. He is a fellow of the American Psychological Association's Division 56 (Trauma). His special interests include assessment, treatment, and training regarding trauma, loss, performance enhancement, and problem behaviors.

Toby Kleinman, J.D.

Toby Kleinman is a New Jersey attorney and partner in the law firm of Adler & Kleinman and has consulted in legal cases in over 40 states. She is an Associate Editor of the *Journal of Child Custody,* and has published articles in the *New Jersey Law Journal.* She is also a director of the advisory board to the Leadership Council on Child Abuse and Interpersonal Violence (LC), has served as the Professional Liaison to APA's Division 56, and has been voted New Jersey Super Lawyer. She has been invited as a keynote speaker at various conferences and has trained family court judges, as well as lecturing at several colleges and appearing as a guest expert on network television.

Eli Newberger, M.D.

Dr. Newberger is a pediatrician who is on the faculty at the Harvard Medical School and is Founder and Medical Director of the Child Protection Program. He is the author of many influential works on child abuse. From his research and practice he has derived a philosophy that focuses on the strength and resilience of parent-child relationships, and he has a practice oriented to compassion and understanding rather than blame and punishment. He has now retired from Boston's Children's Hospital's Harvard Clinic (1970–2000) as he continues his work protecting children as a consultant around the world. Dr. Newberger is also an amazing musician.

David L. Shapiro, Ph.D.

Dr. Shapiro is the author of *Malpractice in Psychology* and *Forensic Psychology Assessment,* among other publications. He consults on both criminal and civil cases, involving assessment of competency, assessment, and prediction of risk for violent behavior, neuropsychological screening, assessment of post-traumatic stress disorders, the psychological and neuropsychological aspects of head trauma, and many other topics.

Dr. Shapiro maintains an independent practice of forensic psychology, and is a Professor at the Center for Psychological Studies at Nova Southeastern University in Ft. Lauderdale, FL where he teaches courses in forensic assessment, professional ethics, and criminal law. He is also conducting research on the Power and Control Inventory (PIC), an innovative approach to the assessment of batterers.

Lenore E.A. Walker, Ed.D., A.B.P.P.

Dr. Walker is a Professor at Nova Southeastern University Center for Psychological Studies and coordinator of the Clinical Forensic Psychology Concentration for doctoral students training to be clinical psychologists. Her graduate students are trained in gender violence areas including battered women and children. Together, with her students, she has developed trauma specific psychotherapy programs in the jails, prisons, and juvenile detention centers.

She frequently testifies as a psychological expert witness in Family Law and Civil Law cases involving child abuse and battered women in courts around the country. Dr. Walker specializes in work with victims of interpersonal violence, and particularly with battered women and abused children.

Dr. Walker is Executive Director of the Domestic Violence Institute with affiliate centers around the world, as well as being the author of 18 books and articles. She is currently President of the American Academy of Couple and Family Psychology of the American Board of Professional Psychology. She does training workshops all over the world about prevention, psychotherapy, legal cases, and public policy initiatives for abused women and children, and is often invited as a keynote speaker on these topics.

Garland Waller

Producer, writer, and educator, Garland Waller began her producing career with the nationally syndicated TV show, *The World of People.* She has produced a wide array of award winning documentaries, not least of all her groundbreaking work *Small Justice: Little Justice in America's Family Courts.* The film was widely praised and the winner of "Best Social Documentary" at the New York International Independent Film and Video Festival in 2001 and the Award for Excellence in media by the 8th International Conference in Family Violence. Her previous film, *Debating Richard Gardner,* exposed the unscientific and sometimes ridiculous tenets of Dr. Gardner's theories about Parental Alienation Syndrome.

Ms. Waller is currently an Assistant Professor in the Department of Television and Film at Boston University.

Hon. Ginger Lerner Wren, J.D.

Judge Lerner Wren was the first judge to sit on the Mental Health Court in Broward County, Florida. At her urging, women who would typically not respond to volunteering for the mental health court began to come, especially as they learned to take responsibility for their own healing. Conducting her courtroom in a trauma-informed manner, she was able to motivate the people in her courtroom to make important changes in their lives. Judge Lerner Wren was one of the Commissioners chosen to be on President George Bush's New Freedom Mental Health Commission in 2002.

In Appreciation

The Editors express their appreciation to Linda God-dard, Executive Assistant for the Nicholas & Dorothy Cummings Foundation, for her countless hours and tireless dedication in shepherding the publication of this volume.

A note of appreciation is also due Bob Kelley of BobKat Productions who went much farther than the extra mile to assure the fidelity of the recordings of this conference so that this book may accurately reflect its proceedings.

Table of Contents

Preface

Nicholas A. Cummings, Ph.D., Sc.D.

For those who have traversed the "Family Court Hell," the information in this volume will be jarringly familiar. For those who are not familiar with what goes on in our family courts, you need to be forewarned. You may unexpectedly be one of several million Americans who each year find themselves unsuspectingly involved in domestic disputes without having an iota of foreknowledge what is about to engulf them, especially if there are children involved.

Domestic disputes typically are contentious and often even ugly. This book goes beyond that, addressing rather a broken system that victimizes those who find themselves haplessly involved. Before reading on, it would be helpful for you to get a preview of what exactly is broken.

First and foremost, the family courts are grounded in the absurd premise that joint custody is always preferable. This results all too frequently in a parent who has been physically and/or sexually abusing the child getting joint custody. Try to imagine, if you can, how a child must feel having to spend half of every year with the parent who cruelly beat or sexually molested him or her.

Secondly, the family courts hold that custody is best given to the biological parent regardless. Too often this results in a child having to live with an addict or a sociopath, or even a felon over and above a responsible and loving foster parent. This may seem too egregious to be believable; I can attest it is not. One morning a case was convened in which I was involved. The family court judge was ruling on a case that had been adjudicated. It involved an African American family of three children, all under age seven, who had been living with the grandparents while the father was serving a two year prison sentence, his second. The mother was serving a life term for murder. In spite of the deeply concerned grandmother's pleas, the judge awarded the children to the father who was obviously not interested in the children, but in the three monthly state child support pay checks he would be receiving. The grandmother dissolved into tears at the verdict as she pleaded with the judge to reconsider. "Your Honor, he will surely do something to go back to prison." The judge, a seemingly maternal looking woman, coldly responded, "Then Madam, you might get the children back." When the grandmother continued in her hysterical distress, the judge ordered the bailiff to forcefully remove her from the courtroom. This entire heart-rending episode took less than ten minutes. My sixty years of practice in which I had thought I had seen everything did not protect me from becoming tearful and shaken.

Thirdly, children have no rights in family court. They are not allowed to testify and they are forced to filter their story through court appointed "expert" psychologists for whom their forensic practice is a cash cow, perpetuating itself by always concluding in what the family courts want to hear: joint custody is best for this child. Attempts to address the lack of children's legal rights are consistently ignored. Only in Israel, and just quite recently, do children have the right to speak.

The breaks in the system go on. As number four, consider that women are usually not believed. The court seems unaware that a sexual psychopathic father is just that: a psychopath who by definition is charming, a facile and believable liar, and seemingly a reasonable and concerned parent. In contrast the mother, who is distraught over the abuse of her children and is desperately trying to protect them, comes across as hysterical, unreasonable, and uncooperative. The courts are taken in as they award the egregious father full custody because the mother is seemingly too unstable. This is an all too common verdict.

There are many more manifestations of a broken system, but I will mention just one more. The courts have bought into the parent alienation syndrome, a rather obtuse concept that only our forensic head shrinks could have conceived. A child at times will side with the offending parent out of fear and awe. This parent, usually the father, has all the money, power, and prestige in the community, while the mother is jobless, fearful, and helpless. The child decides to keep sustaining the abuse in exchange for aligning oneself with power. This perverse situation will become clear as you read on.

And to comprehend the magnitude of the breaks in the system, you must read on. Brace yourself.

Introduction

Janet L. Cummings, Psy.D.

My name is Janet Cummings and I am a survivor of the Family Court Hell. I am also the President of the Nicholas & Dorothy Cummings Foundation that is proud to be the cosponsor of this incisive conference that has brought together this impressive array of dedicated, national leaders. The Cummings Foundation, along with our cosponsor, the National Alliance of Professional Psychology Providers, is grateful to each of them for their incredible many years of commitment to rectifying the flaws in our family court system. Their latest manifestation in a series of many others is that they have agreed to forego a well-deserved speakers fee so that you, our audience, can attend this conference free of charge, and very importantly a book will emerge that will be widely circulated by the Cummings Foundation to the Congress of the United States and several thousand leaders in areas related to the family court system.

I wish to welcome this remarkably enthusiastic audience. Some of you are fellow survivors of the Family Court Hell. We look forward to your participation. It is an honor that so many judges are in attendance, along with psychologists and social workers. And, looking into the near future, I welcome all the readers of the book that is to follow.

At lunch on the second day, we will have the privilege of viewing the important film, *No Way Out But One,* produced by the prize-winning documentary director Garland Waller. She is generously allowing the Cummings Foundation to reproduce this engrossing film so as to be distributed to the Congress along with the book that is to follow.

This conference will follow the format of keynote presentations, followed by panel discussions and audience participation. It is intended to be an active meeting with all the presentations and subsequent discussions being recorded for inclusion in the forthcoming book.

This conference has been two years in the making, co-chaired by world renown Dr. Lenore Walker and the Cummings Foundation's Dorothy Cummings, the effort was graced by the enthusiasm of the invited presenters, but saddened by the sometimes active, but more often under-handed opposition of the entrenched interests. But we are now all here, enthusiastic and ready to proceed. Please welcome our first speaker, Dr. Lenore Walker.

Chapter 1
Seven Deadly Sins in the Family Court System

Lenore E. Walker, Ed.D., A.B.P.P.
(As transcribed from her original conference presentation and published with the permission of the speaker)

I am sorry that I have to sit. As some of you know, I had a very serious muscle disorder for about six months from statin drugs, so I am still healing from it, and standing is not one of the things I can do very easily for any length of time. So I am going to do my talk sitting and struggling with all the papers and everything, but I am so excited to be here.

As Dr. Janet Cummings said, this conference has been in planning for over a year, and I want to thank all my wonderful speakers, who have all agreed to participate in this conference at no cost. There are no fees that are being paid. So you can imagine, we have the passionate as well as the brilliant thinkers who are going to be speaking with you. We purposefully put together people from the legal profession and people from the mental health profession because we constantly point fingers at each other when we look at the problem, saying: Well, if only the evaluator was better or if only the judge was better or if only the lawyer was a better lawyer or even if only one of the parties could afford a lawyer or an evaluator. And that is true. But I think it is a much bigger problem than the individual professions themselves, and so I titled my talk "The Seven Deadly Sins in the Family Court System" because I really want to point out what some of those problems are.

The fact is, there are a lot of custody evaluators who should not be working in the courts. There is no doubt that some of my own professionals are putting a shame and a blight on the mental health system. Yet, I know most of them are good people and they try very hard to do a good job. So those of you who are doing that work, we are failing. And I consider myself failing. I do the best I can do, but I do not have all the tools that I need, and I really do not have all the answers by myself. And I know that there are a lot of good judges, and I know that there are a lot of judges that ought to get off the bench, or they certainly should not be sitting in court, because they do not have the temperament and they do not have the knowledge. I am thrilled that we have so many judges that have come to this conference. But, you know, most of the conferences that I do all over the world, judges won't come. Now, they will come if I come to them. If I go into court and I go into their court conferences or I go into the judicial college conferences, they will show up there. But this isn't to empower one profession. This is an interactive approach, and we have to learn together to find the solutions to protect children.

The same thing for doctors: We do not have too many doctors who will come to these conferences. We have Dr. Eli Newberger who is going to be speaking with us, a pediatrician for many, many years, who has been working on these cases. But his colleagues in medicine do not come to the conferences.

Mental health professionals need the Continuing Education units and they come. And I do go to doctor trainings where they get their CE credits. So they do get the information. But the fact is, we are not talking with each other to try to find the solutions. We have some recent research—and I am not going to give you all the statistics—but this morning I am going to give you a broad outline of where I see the problems are. Then our speakers are going to, one at a time, be able to tell you from their perspective, from the work that they have been doing in the field, working in this area, and knowing the academic literature. I tried to find people who knew both who could give us that combination, because it is not just enough to see it from our own small perspective; we have to know what other people are doing all over the world. This is not just a problem in the United States. My husband, Dr. David Shapiro, and I do training every year in Spain. We have been doing this for the last seven years, and the problem is there. I have been training in Israel; the problem is there. And in countries as you will hear other people. I was in Hong Kong last year working on a case, and the problem is there. You will hear from Judge Marjorie Fields after me, who was training in other countries as well, and I am sure other people also have. So it is not fair to say it is individuals' faults. As did Janet, I am going to ask you to please suspend your judgmental beliefs for the next two days. Do not think about what you want it to be or what it could be if somebody else did such-and-such, but think about where am I in this area, what do I have to offer, and what do I have to think about as we put it all together. And, hopefully, by tomorrow afternoon when we have all the panelists together on a big reactor panel, we can come up with some ideas, some solutions.

I just want to remind us all that just this week the courts in Virginia fined Virginia Tech millions and millions and millions of dollars as they found the university negligent by failing to protect those children on that campus. Remember, they are people's children who are on that campus.

I say this conference throws down the gauntlet. We are going to put on the record what is happening and why that is bad for children, emphasizing that we must become part of the solution. We may have to force a solution here in this country, and we may have to go to courts with this, as other people have been going to the courts. Judge Fields, whom you will hear from afterwards, was one of the pioneers in New York City as a legal-aid attorney who took the city to court back in the 1970s for the failure to protect battered women and their children. So she is still fighting and still feisty. We still have civil rights attorneys, as this is a civil rights issue. This is an issue of failure to protect women, children, and some men as well. So let's talk a little bit about where we're going.

I just want to tell you some of the figures that I have been learning as we have been inviting people to the conference. There are some studies that have not even been published yet. There is a wonderful study by the National Institute of Justice, whose principal investigator was Dan Saunders. He found that education was helpful in changing attitudes, but that there are attitudes that still exist with judges and with custody evaluators. He found that a large percentage of them do not believe women when they claim that there is abuse in the family and do not believe the children when they claim abuses in the family. And for those who do believe what the person is saying in their court, they do not think it matters that much when deciding access to these children. That's a national shame and that's something we really have to change. Why it exists that way is what we are going to explore so that we can really figure out some of the changes needed.

A more recent study done by Dr. Geraldine Stahly in the California Protective Parents Coalition is even more significant. Eighty-one percent of the hundreds of women that they studied in their research came to the court after a divorce had been filed with a custody dispute. When they came to the court, they had always been the custodial parent, and over fifty percent of them left the court with no access to their children. That's a shame. It should not be. It should not be, for the sake of the children. Those of us who are child psychologists know that taking the child away from the mother because the court does not believe the mother, and where there is abuse in the family, is totally destructive for the children. So why? How does it happen?

1. The First Deadly Sin in the Family Court System.

The first of the seven deadly sins are the systematic errors in the court system itself. It is flawed. No matter how good any of us can be, those errors are going to prevent us from protecting children. And that is really what this is all about.

The first problem in family court is the presumptions that we have to work within in most states. I could start back even earlier and say the first, biggest problem is that we allow state by state by state to make these kinds of rules about access to children. Perhaps we ought to look at a national standard. Perhaps one of the things we need to look at is seeing if we can get Congress to address the issue, although I am not exactly sure that the current Congress can do anything like that. But it would be important to get them to act especially because of the war on women that seems to be being fought daily. But they could not even extend the Violence Against Women Act without extending it with problems. Be that as it may, it may still be easier to persuade one legislative body like the Congress rather than fifty state legislative bodies to remove some of these presumptions that are so dangerous for these children.

The first issue is that in most of the states, the sets of family laws have some sort of clause that talks about reunification, or if not reunification, some talk of keeping the family together. It is in the dependency statutes of the family court statutes that it is in the states' best interests to keep the family together. I teach a course in psychology and family law in our forensic psychology concentration at Nova, and in that course I start it off every semester with these mostly young, very bright, eager people at the age where they are all looking for marital partners, or at least some kind of partner, and I start off by saying to them: Marriage is not about love. Marriage is a contract between you and somebody else and the state, and it is in the state's best interests to have the two of you take care of each other. The exception, of course, is if you are of the same sex. Then that is not in the state's best interests, although if they were smart enough, the legislators would get off of all their other politics and realize that even this would fit within the areas of why we have all of these laws surrounding marriage and dissolution of marriage. That is, it is in the state's best interests because if you take care of your partner and your children, then the state does not have to do it. And that is just the bottom line in our legal documents.

We also now have the presumption that shared parental responsibility, or joint custody, or any other name by which you call the giving equal access to children by both parents, is in the best interests of the child. Well, as a scientist and a psychologist who knows the literature very well, there is not one empirical scientific study that says that it is in the child's best interest to be with both parents when you have one parent who has an abnormal ability to go after power and control and abuse. There is not any study that says that a child has a right to be abused. So that presumption needs to be taken out of the legal systems, in my opinion. This presumption, for those of you who are not that familiar with it, means that this is what is supposedly in the best interests of the child, and anyone who wants to change it, has the burden of proof to prove why they want to change it. And in most states, the burden of proof is not just that it isn't good or it isn't in the best interests of the child, but in many of the states that I work in, you have to demonstrate that it is detrimental to the best interests of the child or you have to demonstrate that it will cause irreparable harm to the child. These are extremely high burdens to prove, especially when you are doing an evaluation with children that may appear to be extremely resilient at that particular moment, as well as when you are doing an evaluation and the parent who has asked you to do the evaluation does not have the financial resources to go further with demonstrating that in the court. And another systemic error, which is really a violation of due process rather than just a systemic error, is the trend in family courts not to have court reporters take down and transcribing all of the information going on in the court. Especially so if the parties do not have the money to pay for transcribing. We will talk more about this later, but the last several cases that I testified in, I was shocked to find there was not even a tape recorder recording it. It was only the court (i.e., the judge's notes). I don't imply that there was a problem with the judge taking those notes, but that only lets it be seen through one person's eyes rather than having the whole transcript in front of appellate courts that might be able to remedy some of the mistakes that could be made. However, I think that Judge Fields and Judge Lerner Wren are going to tell you that the appellate courts rarely reverse decisions in these kinds of cases.

The next presumption, which is one that we find very much to the detriment of children, is that the friendliest parent is going to be the best parent to get custody if shared custody is not appropriate. So if the abuser, who oftentimes is quite charming in the courtroom, comes in and presents himself as being extremely friendly while the mom, who is being a protective mother and does not want to allow the children to be with the parent whom she believes is abusing the child because the child tells her so and does not want to be with the abusive parent, then the court sees her as not the friendly parent. And so now the presumption is, it is the other person who gets the custody of the child no matter who is the real "psychological parent" of the child. And this is another presumption that really is well-meaning but needs to be thrown out because it is not working properly.

And then the last one is the presumption that the biological parent is always the best parent, which is an old throwback. This presumption does not understand that parenting through adoption or through marriage may be the best parents of the child and it may be in the best interests of the child to be with that parent. That parent, both in dependency court and in child custody cases, rarely gets a fair chance in the courtroom without spending sometimes hundreds of thousands of dollars. The amount of money that is spent in these cases is really a shame. There are also contradictions. These are just some of the presumptions that we face daily when we are in family court.

There are also contradictions that really have no answer because they are both very strongly held beliefs that may be contrary to each other. There can be the strongly held belief in the same person that the best interests of the child should be primary and at the same time privacy rights should be primary and we should not open up the doors of our family and show our secrets. And so people fight for their privacy and at the same time fight for the best interests of the child. Well, you cannot always see what is in the best interests of the child. And I am not so sure that "best interests" is a very measurable standard as a psychologist that has tried to measure best interests, because what is good for one child may not be good for a child at another age. And so that standard itself needs a lot of research. We can at least ask: Does it make sense? It sounds good and we like what it says. But is that really the best standard? And, furthermore, is it the best standard when we have abuse allegations in the family? So I present to you, it probably is not.

The last area of due process violations I want to mention before I move on to the second deadly sin is the issue of money and the courts. If you don't have money, you don't get justice in most of our legal system, and that is true in family court as well. Some have suggested that perhaps the court should hire evaluators. But having worked in courts where they do have their own evaluators, I suggest to you that that is not necessarily a good suggestion, because the courts will cut costs immediately on paying evaluators. So the people who end up doing this work may not be well-enough trained and may not have the sophistication or the understanding because the bottom line is that, very few cases of people who have children and will get a divorce ever go before the court for a custody determination.

2. Stereotypical Bias in Adjudicators and Evaluators.

We make all our rules, all our laws, all of our psychology guidelines based on the fact that these are going to be "normal" families. But normal families tend to settle their differences on their own. The people who come to the court for guidance are the people that cannot settle it on their own. It may be a nice pipedream that we can do the settlement for them through a custody evaluation. But it may not be possible that strangers, who come into people's lives with predetermined biases of their own, can really make those kinds of determinations in perhaps maybe the 10% of the cases that get into the court and that need the court's attention. And those 10% so overload the court docket that it is almost impossible to give the attention that the cases need to be able to be settled fairly. It takes me over two to three days to do a comprehensive evaluation and then another month or two to let it settle, to look up things, to go to the research, to write up a report to really get it right. I then go back to my clients, have them look at the information, to make sure I heard it correctly or I interpreted it correctly, for another 10 to 20 hours working on one of these evaluations. And the court expects to be able to do it in less than a day or two. It simply cannot happen that way. So the system itself is flawed in expectations that just are not going to happen. I can tell you, in one of the cases that I testified in not too long ago, the judge gave each side fifteen minutes. How can you present your case in fifteen minutes? And when something came out on cross-examination that had not been told before, the court refused to hear it because time was up. The person used their time up. That is not justice. That is not due process. And that is not doing right by children.

We also want to look at evidence. All my lawyer friends love to talk about the evidentiary rules. So we have had to learn as psychologists, what are the evidentiary rules? Well, evidence is usually based on facts. Women don't think that way. We have plenty of research, psychological research, to know that women mix facts with our feelings. That is how we live. So when we are being asked to separate facts from emotions in the court, it is very difficult to do, and the legal profession does not understand that or does not want to understand that. They want to try to separate them out. Well, there are ways around that. You can change evidence. We did that with battered-woman syndrome in cases where women kill their abuser in what they claim was self-defense. They were only supposed to look at that particular act and, according to the evidence, the criminal codes in most states at that time. We went before the legislatures and eventually, often case by case, and demonstrated that you could not look at just one episode. Domestic violence is a pattern. It is a pattern of an abuse of power and control. Sometimes it is with actual physical violence, sometimes with actual sexual violence, and sometimes you do not need to have the actual violence because, like bullies in the schoolyard, threats are enough to scare someone. And that is what it is about. It is not about just one factor of one act. So when you get stuck with evidentiary issues that are not being admitted into the court because allegedly they are not accurate, then we have to go back to the legislatures and change what the evidence requirements are.

We also have a problem with things that are not written down. Women who are raising young children often do not have the time, the facilities, or the resources to write everything down that happens. And when you are emotionally upset, it is also more difficult to write it down until it sort of settles for you. So oftentimes women do not come in with the "He did this on this date and he did this in that hour and he did this at another time." And so, if it is not written down, as I have been told in courtrooms, we don't have to believe it; only in writing do we believe it. And sometimes the batterer understands that and comes in with pages and pages and pages of all of his problems with what she has done. Not that she has not done it, but the inequality in what the evidence is in front of the court makes it very difficult to be able to come up with an accurate finding.

And then the last part, which is, I think, even more important for psychologists, is that we do not always understand that children are resilient, and when they know they are going to have to spend time with a person who may be also abusing them, they will concentrate on the loving part of that relationship and not on the abusive part of the relationship. And they are more resilient and can cover it up, and you will not know the truth from the child unless you really are willing to take the time and the appropriate way of interviewing and talking with the children. I do believe that a child not having a voice in the courtroom is one of the systemic errors in family court cases. Children should be represented. They should have legal representation.

I just heard that California has passed a law or just a rule, saying that the judges can now talk to the children. Well, I think that is great for some judges, but I am terrified with some other judges. So, as I understand it, psychologists are now going to be the ones who are going to be training the judges. Good luck. I suspect this is a good idea, but I have a feeling that this kind of a solution is not enough. Lawyers know how to talk to judges and judges know how to talk to lawyers, but the rest of us do the best we can, and sometimes the judge makes it easy for us and sometimes the judge really makes it very difficult because they have a million rules and can cut us off at any point that they want to. And sometimes the children can feel really comfortable with a judge, and some of the judges that you hear today, I think, would be fine with kids. But some of the judges that I have been in front of—I do not want to be in front of them. If I have to go back in their courtroom, I am not so happy about it. Okay.

So the last piece is with parenting plans. This is the latest that we have in Florida, and I again have to tell you that having non-psychologists make a parenting plan with the parents that cannot agree about anything else, and with one party who wants more power and control and will take it away, is going to be doomed to failure as well. These parenting plans are no better than what the old court did in saying, "You're the parent; you have the responsibility of deciding how you are going to parent that child." And by trying to force the parents into parenting plans is taking away the opportunity and the power of the parent to supervise children. It is not so bad when children are young, but as they get older, their taking away the parental authority is only going to get the children into more difficulty in their having to go to other people for the authority to determine whether they are right or wrong.

Lastly, still on only the second sin, is the fact that the best parent in an abusive situation may be one parent, with the other parent having no contact with the child. Why? Because we know enough as psychologists that if the child has been in any way affected by the abuse, then that child will have symptoms of post-traumatic stress disorder. They may not have full-blown PTSD, but they will have symptoms of it. Post-traumatic stress disorder repeats itself even when that parent is not there. There are triggers that trigger the effects, and the parent, usually himself, will become the trigger. As a result, the relationship between the child and that parent will never be free from producing the PTSD symptoms. And so it may be dooming that child to never have a relationship with that parent by forcing the parenting at the time that the dissolution is occurring or the evaluation is occurring. And the statistics are pretty scary. Very few courts will refer and very few custody evaluators will be sensitive to this fact. By the way, custody evaluators and the courts in the Saunders study I mentioned earlier have similar opinions, whereas domestic violence advocates and legal-aid attorneys have much more similar opinions to believing that children and women are being abused than judges and custody evaluators. So we have to somehow make it understood that the majority of the cases that are going to be coming before the courts will have abuse in those cases, and what we have to be able to sort out is: How do you figure that out?

In summary, the second deadly sin is not ridding ourselves—and that means all of us—of our stereotypical biases that we come to when we do an evaluation or when we try to help adjudicate these kinds of cases. And if I had more time, I would spend it with you talking about gender issues and about civil rights issues and the worldwide issues around gender that are being studied that we do not hear very much about in the United States. But around the world, there are commissions on gender. There are in the cabinets of governments, areas that look at the systematic biases against people because of their gender, and that is something that happens because it is women who are being disbelieved. It is protective moms who are being disbelieved in these cases, as well as the children. You can see that some of what we need to look at is changing the stereotypes of who is the good-enough woman, who is the good-enough mother, who is the good-enough father, who is the good-enough man, what do these sex roles and gender roles have to do with this? That influences the kinds of decisions that are being made, both in the custody evaluation and in the courts. I cannot tell you how many evaluations I have read where the evaluator takes the exact same behavior that he or she sees in the man and in the woman, and then writes a comment about how strong and how wonderful it is that the man is doing X, Y, and Z and how bad it is that the woman is doing the same exact behavior. That is gender bias. And when I am asked by the boards of psychology to review the complaints, that is the first thing I scan the report for, is the language that is being used. I know that Dr. Toby Kleinman is going to talk about some of that language tomorrow in her talk, as it is critical in the way it influences our language and influences our thinking. Our thinking influences how we conduct these evaluations and what we do with the results of them.

3. Ignorance of Child Development.

The third deadly sin is ignorance of child development. Anybody who does not clearly understand the theories of child development—and that means lawyers and it means psychologists or other mental health evaluators—should not be doing these evaluations. If you do not understand age appropriateness, how can you understand what the child is saying? Is what the child is saying consistent with the child's "style." Is it consistent with the research on the child's age?

- Children "talk" through play. You need observation skills.
- Children "talk" through physical symptoms.
- Children "talk" to other children.
- Children "talk" through drawings.
- Children "talk" through behavior.
- Children "talk" by answering age appropriate questions.

4. Ignorance of Child Abuse.

If you do not understand child development, you miss what they are saying, you miss what they need, and that is a huge problem in the cases, and not only in the lack of child development knowledge, but also the ignorance of child abuse. David and I just finished a case where psychologists wrote in the report and testified on the witness stand that this child could not have been harmed because she was three years old and there were no physical injuries to the child. So there was some sex play, but that does not harm children unless the child is physically injured by it. That is total ignorance. I mean, he should lose his license for being a psychologist, and the saddest thing is he was hired by the Board of Psychology in that state and offered that opinion.

Children have conflicting feelings in their love and dislike of the abusive parent versus the non-offending parent. A potentially sexually abusing parent may precede the abuse with "grooming behavior" that prepares the child to be abused. There is variability in the form abuse takes, and the non-offending parent may need to be protected. Children have unrealistic expectations about other's ability to read abuse. In order for the child to disclose, the child must feel safe from continued abuse. There may be co-occurring disorders such as PTSD and ADHD resulting in the abuse being missed by the evaluator.

Children disclose in a variety of different ways. There are wonderful guidelines that are produced by the American Professional Society of the Abuse of Children (ABSAC) and some other organizations. The American Bar Association's (ABA) guidelines are sort of wishy-washy, but they can at least help us a little bit in how to do it. Judges need to learn what is in a good psychological report, lawyers need to know what is in a good psychological report, and they need to not hire their friends or their colleagues, but they need to hire the people who are right for that particular situation. We need to be able to help the legal systems and the psychologists. We have to not just go after the business ourselves, but be able to help our colleagues who are properly trained for a particular case to be able to do that case.

5. Domestic Violence.

Deadly sin number five is ignorance of domestic violence. I am not going to spend a lot of time on it because I know other people are as well. But the bottom line is: you are not going to learn about domestic violence in one course or one CE workshop. You have to understand it. You have to be able to understand the literature, do reading in the area, and educate yourselves in the effects of domestic violence, because it is counterintuitive. It is not what it looks like on the surface, and you have to really spend the time and understand what the typical kinds of behaviors are. When I do my training, all of a sudden students look up and say: "But—but—but, Dr. Walker, these men all are saying the same thing or doing the same thing and they do not know each other. How did that happen?" Well, I suspect it happens because of our socialization of people, not just our own family socialization in our homes, but also our socialization in the media, and we are going to see a wonderful film tomorrow.

There is much misinterpretation of tests. I can tell you they are giving the wrong tests. Millon Clinical Multiaxial Inventory (MCMI) tests are lovely because they are short and they are cheap to use and most people can read them, but the fact is, you are not supposed to give that test to anybody who does not already have a psychological problem. Those of us who know the test know that it over-diagnoses pathology. So it should not be used in custody evaluations. Now, they write all kinds of things saying it should be because they are entrepreneurs and selling their tests.

But the bottom line is, the tests that are being used in custody evaluations are poor, all of them are poor, but some are better than others. And then not only do we give wrong tests, but we also misinterpret the tests. Okay.

You must be aware of the duplicity of the batterer's behavior, which can resemble Dr. Jekyll/Mr. Hyde. More often than not they are real charmers. People heal from PTSD and Battered Women's Syndrome (BWS) in stages and custody evaluations may occur at the anger stage. Often BWS women must survive by deception, omission, or even outright lying, behavior that may be totally misunderstood by the evaluator as survival.

6. Children Have NO Legal Standing.

Number six deadly sin is the fact that children have no legal standing in court. I do not think it is enough to just give them voice. I think they need to be represented by lawyers, not by guardians *ad litem*. The difference, very quickly for those who do not know, is that most guardians *ad litem* are not lawyers, while some are. Even though they are not, their responsibility is to protect the best interests of the child. Lawyers protect the child's wishes. Now that does not mean the child's wishes are going to be granted, but it means the court will learn what the child's true wishes are. So the lawyer should be the person who has confidentiality, can protect the child, does not have to tell, as we have to, as we have the responsibility of reporting child abuse.

I have not talked about the deadly sin of getting so many courts involved. You have the family court involved. Then you have an allegation of domestic violence and an allegation of child abuse, so you have a mandatory report. You have to report to dependency court in the larger cities. Then you find out that somebody has been arrested for juvenile delinquency, so now you have a third court that is involved, and you have the father who may have assaulted the mother, so now you have criminal court involved. There has been a movement towards unified family courts. I have not found them to be particularly helpful. And I think that is because it helps you not have to go court, court, court, court, and some of the judges are excellent who sit on the family court, but some of them are not. So it comes right back to who is doing the work and whether they want to be there and not just assigned to it. Okay?

One of my very close friends, who is a retired Israeli judge, was appointed by the Israeli Supreme Court to the commission that rewrote every law from the children's perspective as well as that of the adult's perspective. The children were given legal standing, and once you give legal standing to children everywhere, they become a person and they have rights and it becomes an important perspective to keep in mind. She said the process took them about five or six years to do, but she claims that it does make a difference in what happens to the children there, although not enough to change everything, but it is a step.

7. Few Incentives for System Change.

The last one is the bottom line: There are few incentives to change the system, and we have got to find what incentives will get the system changing, get it moving. We have got to make sure that there is due process in the system, and we need to continue the wonderful court-watching that we have with advocates in some of our different communities. Unfortunately, many of the communities do not have court-watchers, especially when you are going through, as Janet so aptly named it, "family court hell," because maybe you can climb out of it, but you are forever scarred by it. The scars are there and they are wreaking havoc on our population. I have been doing this for almost forty years and I ask, why hasn't it changed? Well, I think one of the big reasons why it has not changed is that we are raising new generations of children that are scarred by abuse and by domestic violence. Go into the jails and the prisons and interview women. Eighty-five to ninety percent of those women all have experienced trauma of one sort or another. Many of them turn to substance abuse because of the trauma that they have experienced. Many of them get themselves in trouble with the criminal courts because of the abusers that they are with. And go into death row and you will not find an inmate there who has not been abused in his life. So if we do not stop this march against children's rights, if we do not stop the abuse that children are being put through in family court right at the beginning when they are very young, I do not believe we are going to be able to stop violence. And every time I gave a talk in the early days, I said I really, really wish that violence will stop at some point in my lifetime. Well, I am getting older, folks, so I think we have got to really move this if it is going to happen in my lifetime.

Thank you very much.

Chapter 2

Domestic Violence Cases are a Major Aspect of the Breakdown of the Family Court

Hon. Marjory D. Fields, J.D.

DR. JANET CUMMINGS: Judge Fields participated in the first lawsuit against New York City courts. And they say you can't sue city hall? Yes, you can. And the court system. She did this for failure to provide adequate services and protect battered women, and this was over 30 years ago. She continues to write and be an advocate for protection for domestic violence victims, adults, and children and is author of *Diversion is Dangerous, Getting Beyond What Did She Do to Provoke Him.*

J udge Fields is one of the good guys or good gals. We will hear some complaints about judges in general. Judges are not all bad, judges can only work within the system that they have, but some have the guts to try and change that system for the better, not just to sit on the bench, making a one-minute entry after another. Judge Fields has dedicated her life to the victims and the underserved, not to getting wealthy off a system that has become very, very lucrative for attorneys and mental health professionals. So please welcome the Honorable Marjory Fields.

JUDGE FIELDS: Can you see me over the podium? That was my uncle's comment when I took the bench and he came to watch, and he said, "Judge, am I going to be able to see you over the top of the bench?" My predecessor had been a very large man, and the chair I inherited was concave, and I kind of disappeared into it. We got a new chair, but it took a while.

Family courts are really no worse than any other courts. They are a part of a society and a legal system that, as the distinguished and esteemed psychologist Lenore Walker just described to you, has a pervasive gender bias. I use the "esteemed psychologist" designation for Dr. Walker because there is an article in the current issue of the *Journal of the American Academy of Psychiatry and the Law* which designates her that way. The article is "The Parental Alienation Debate Belongs in the Courtroom, Not in DSM-V," and I commend it to you. It is excellent. It is very clear. And it raises some valid issues about parental alienation and the expense and distraction that it creates from the reality, because you end up trying that issue instead of the issues in the case. Also, they conclude with a comment that I thought should be at the beginning, and that is: "Why would we want these conflicted children caught in the middle to be labeled as mentally ill?" And parental alienation syndrome labels a child inappropriately, even if it were a valid diagnosis, which we know it is not.

Family court dysfunction is based in the history of our courts. Family courts started out as juvenile courts to try juvenile delinquency cases, with the idea that, instead of punishing, we would provide services to children. And family courts have always had two goals, two functions, and one is a social-work function and the other is to be a court of law. And these are inconsistent and conflicting, and it creates the ongoing institutional problems that exist there. And the United States Supreme Court has addressed these issues, and as the judges and lawyers will know, the first and most important case was Gault in which the Supreme Court said: It's a juvenile delinquency case. Just because you are going to help this child, does not mean you can function without all the constitutional and statutory due process requirements that an adult in a criminal court would have, except the jury. And it is possible that someday the court will decide we need juries in juvenile delinquency cases also. But taking a child and putting that child into a juvenile detention center or a juvenile home, secured, doors locked, where this child was going to get services is, the Supreme Court said, a deprivation of liberty, and, therefore, even though you are not putting the child in a jail or prison, that child gets due process rights.

The Court also addressed the issue of due process in Stanley against Illinois, which was a case that dealt with the father's right to be the custodian of his children when he had not done anything wrong, except he was not married to their mother and she died. The State of Illinois removed Mr. Stanley's children from his care only because he was their unmarried father. There was no other allegation. And the Supreme Court said "no" to that as well. So we had that, and then there's Offer against Dunston, which is the case in which the Supreme Court said: If you are going to terminate parental rights because there has been child abuse or neglect and that parent has failed to engage in services and the children need stability and have to be freed for adoption, that you cannot use the lowest standard of proof. This is our general standard in family courts, which is preponderance of the evidence, so it is just slightly more. It is the lowest standard—you have to have clear and conclusive evidence, not as high as the criminal standard, which is beyond a reasonable doubt. But, again, that was the United States Supreme Court saying to family courts: You are a court of law. You are not a social-work institution. But the historical social-work function and role is a hangover that lingers in the family courts.

Historically, we have seen the family courts go through a name change. Unfortunately, name changes do not mean that we have had institutional change. Our favorite joke in New York is that the Child Protective Services Agency has been renamed about four times. You can tell a person's age by how he or she refers to it. So if you still call it BCW, Bureau of Child Welfare, we know you are an antique. I think it is the Agency for Child Welfare now, ACW. I am not sure what its current name is. But I went through several names, but for some reason, since my original name was Bureau of Child Welfare, that is how I think of it. A brilliant trial lawyer who practiced in front of me and represented children later became a family court judge, and is now the New York City Commissioner in charge of this agency. Whatever its name is, he is wonderful, and I hope that he will be able to make the progressive changes for children that I know he is inclined to make if the budgets let him.

And then there is the matter of budgets. All the courts in the United States are suffering, except the federal courts, I might say. All the state courts in the United States are suffering from budget cuts. We have states in which the courts are only open four days a week instead of five. In New York, our courts are required to close at 4:30. If you have a witness in the stand, that witness cannot finish her sentence. The day is ended. Staff have to leave because there can be no overtime. State legislatures, an equal branch of government with the courts, have cut the budgets, because there are balanced-budget requirements in many states. The money has to be found somewhere, and the courts are one of the places. The courts go to the legislature and the executive every year with a begging bowl. The courts have no bargaining power really when they are dealing with their budget requests. So a lot of the problem in family courts is the historic lower funding level. The money priority has always been the criminal courts, and that is because of the Supreme Court decisions that put very high burdens of speed on the criminal court, as they should when people are in custody. But there is not the same burden of speed when it comes to the children's issues that the family courts deal with.

Recent federal law has changed that to some extent, but we are talking about requiring months, not hours. When it comes to a criminal defendant who is in custody, that defendant must be before a judge for arraignment within 24 hours. That is what the Supreme Court says. So where does the money have to go? It has got to go into the criminal courts. Otherwise we would have to open the jail doors without having the opportunity to consider risk flight from the jurisdiction. This is one of the problems that we could face if this person's right to be released on bail on his own recognizance or the state's right to continue to hold him is not considered.

I am not going to discuss gender bias again. I think Lenore Walker covered that for you, including the recent Saunders, Fowler, and Tollman study.

Historically, domestic violence in my state, New York, was required to go into the family court. That was where we had protection orders starting in 1962, although you could not get one in 1971 when I started practicing in New York, but we had the statute. And if the case was being prosecuted in the criminal courts, then the woman could not get any protection in the family court because the criminal court had the case and family court had no jurisdiction. If she wanted a protection order only and the prosecutor was not taking the case, then she had to go to the family court. And the problem was, she wasn't believed, that she must have provoked him, and there were lots of judges who believed that and said that. Well, that was one of the issues that faced the Women's Movement. There was advocacy for training judges, which I do not necessarily trust, although Dr. Saunders and his team think that domestic violence is a pattern and practice of control and exercise of power and abuse of power and not a single incident. Well, there's the unintended consequence. And I have read decisions in .which judges write that a single act of assault in the course of a high-conflict divorce is not domestic violence because it is not part of a pattern of control. However, it remains to be a criminal offense of assault, which the prosecutor has the right to prosecute. The police have made the arrest. They have probable cause, and it can be prosecuted. In one particular case, the prosecutor not only agreed to charge, but took it to trial and there was an acquittal. The defendant cried on the witness stand. He also did that in the divorce court. And he was very good at being pathetic. And so the jurors acquitted him. Now, the judge in the divorce case in New York is not bound by the acquittal. Had there been a conviction, it would have been proof beyond a reasonable doubt, and the judge could not ignore that finding. In fact, the lawyer could have made what we call a Motion for Summary Judgment and not have to try that again. Because it was already determined beyond a reasonable doubt, there was no issue left on whether or not that assault had taken place. Even though there was medical evidence of torn ligaments in the wife's arm and even though there was probable cause and sufficient cause for the People to prosecute it, the judge found it was not real domestic violence because there had not been other incidents of assault or threatening raised in the case. It was not relevant; it was not necessary. There was only this assault.

So what we had is, judges have now been trained that there is a pattern and, having absorbed that, when there is only one incident of assault, it is not domestic violence anymore. So this is the unintended consequence. So we have to be careful what we do and what we think about the logical extension. Rather than having programs like this to train judges, I believe that it requires good lawyers on a case-by-case basis, walking into the courtroom and presenting the evidence. I could know a great deal about domestic violence and child abuse. I practiced 15 years. Ninety-eight percent of my clients were women complaining of domestic violence because New York was a fault-only divorce jurisdiction until last October. We were the last holdout for no-fault divorce, so everybody had to have a cause of action, and one of them was a continuous course of physical or mental cruelty, and if my clients had the evidence, that is how we got them divorced. I knew a lot about it. Fifteen hundred divorces a year for 15 years. As I say, my experience is anecdotal, but it is kind of vast.

In addition, I read the literature. I worked with others in New York and across the U.S. I went to legal services offices in 36 states. I trained legal services lawyers about domestic violence. I testified before state legislatures. Pennsylvania was the next state to adopt protection orders. I went to testify in Harrisburg before the state legislature. I testified before Congress. So I know a lot about it. I have read about it. I practiced it. But when you put me on the bench, I could not decide your case because you had the evidence; I didn't. You had to give me the evidence. That is true of every judge. You educate judges case by case. I learned about child abuse case by case and also the literature and from the expert witnesses, one of whom is here today, Dr. Daniel Kessler. He left me in New York. He left us in the lurch and came out here 21 years ago as one of the boys in Phoenix.

But you cannot educate a judge and then expect a judge to decide the case if you do not do what we call "make a record," present the evidence. As Dr. Walker said: We always want the evidence; show us. And if you have a jury, you have to show the jurors too. So in family court, we sit without juries, but you cannot expect us, no matter how well-read or experienced we are, to decide your case if we have not seen the evidence in this specific case. And the burden is preponderance of the evidence in the family courts. So that is not terrible. In 48 of the 50 states, the statutes provide that when there is domestic violence, the domestic violence offender cannot have custody of the child. South Dakota and Utah, I think, are the two states, if I recall, that do not have that in their statute. However, judges have an enormous amount of discretion, and just as the single act of domestic violence is not domestic violence when it is not part of a pattern, even though it is a criminal assault, a judge can also find that, although there was domestic violence in this family, it did not harm the children, they were not affected. Therefore the offender, who we know has committed acts of domestic violence that have been proven in the court, is still competent to be a joint custodian. Or there is a new fairly recent development that in addition to custody, judges are now doing divided decision-making. So you have a custodial parent who has most of the decision-making, and then the judge decides that the noncustodial parent will be the one who has decision-making over extracurricular activities.

Now, you have two people in front of you who cannot agree about anything and you are going to give one of them part of the decision-making. Now what would you expect to happen? Everything would become an extracurricular activity. So if the custodial parent is in charge of the education decision-making and we have a child who goes to school, what will the child study? And what if the child needs after-school math tutoring, is that educational or is that extracurricular activity? And, Judge, aren't you buying yourself a continued war of post-judgment motions? How many times do you want to see this case again? And are you making your own bed and now you are going to lie in it? Plus, I think that breaking up the decision-making in a situation in which the statute says and the facts you have found say that you have a domestic violence offender here who cannot have custody, you are violating the legislative intent by granting that person educational or extracurricular or medical or vacation decision-making, however you want to divide this.

Dr. Walker said that one of the best things to do would be to have a national family law. Well, once again, we have to be careful what we want. We could get it. Canada has a national family law. It works pretty well there. Three or four years ago, Australia passed a new family custody statute in which there is a presumption of equal time post-separation with each parent. And I have this image of the child being wakened in the middle of the night to switch beds, because you have to sleep 50% of the time in each house. And of course children go to school and parents go to work. How do you calculate the 50% time with each parent? In addition, does anybody who has empathy for children or perhaps anybody who has traveled a great deal have a sense of: What does this child write in its school papers when they want to know, what is your home address? And someone suggested, well, he can put down two. No, the form does not have space for two addresses. It only has space for one. But what do you write down? Or as one child said, "When I go to the other house, I never remember where the spoons are kept."

I practiced law in New York. I spent the legislative session days in the state capital of Albany 150 miles away. I usually took the bus because it was more reliable than the train, although a lot less comfortable. I spent my weekends in a little cottage in the country because my former companion believed his dogs had to go to the country every weekend, and they did. Moving to three different places every week: Where are your gym shoes on the day you have gym? Where is your annotated science textbook?— Which is kind of arcane now because it is probably all in your computer anyway. But I remember spending a time with a friend in Edinburgh who was divorced, and she and her husband split the child's residence. He spent two weeks in each house or maybe even three, but they were only five blocks apart. It was really doable. Plus, his mother traveled for business. So it was excellent for the child to be able to go to the father's home and have that stability, and the father's new wife was a lovely person. In fact, his mother, my friend, was the backup babysitter for the husband and the second wife's new baby. So they got along. I called one year at New Year's and got the son who is now a man about 30 and we chatted, and I said, "Where's your mother?" "Oh, she's at Bob's. She stayed. I came home." So she was continuing to spend New Year's Day with her ex-husband, his second wife, and their three children. So, obviously, it was a good working relationship, and they had made this decision themselves. But one day when he was nine and I was visiting, Bob brought his son back, and a few minutes into the return before the father left, the child said, "I forgot my watch at your house." And the father looked at him and said, "I knew you would forget something." So the burden is on the child to move all his necessary things. Now, obviously, if there is enough money, there might be duplicates. But some things there might not be, like the watch and the gym shoes. So we have to look out for what we get if we get a national law, because it could be the Australian preference for equal time that is not necessarily dispensed with in domestic violence cases. It creates a greater burden in those cases in Australia. We know that from what has happened since the statute passed.

Another problem in family law in many courts is where the divorces are not in the family court, but in the superior court. This is so in New York where, as you remember, divorces are not in family court. So we are dealing with different judges who do not sit in the family court, most of whom did not come from the family court, as I was an exception. In family cases, the trend is now to have balanced decisions. Now, a balanced decision is that you give each of the parents something and that way nobody is going to be angry or if he or she is angry, at least he's got and she's got something that was won in this litigation. The trouble with balanced decisions is that in the course of doing that, you deny the legal remedies to which someone is entitled. If you have proven your case that you are entitled to a certain remedy and the judge's priority is a balanced decision, then, in the course of that, somebody is going to be deprived of legal rights. As for a balanced decision, let me give you an example of a domestic violence case. The family court judge found that the husband had assaulted the wife who was wheelchair-bound. He knocked her out of her chair and she was knocked unconscious. And so the judge in the family court, a woman judge, a former colleague of mine, decided that the woman was entitled to a protection order. That's easy. The order was that the husband was not to strike, menace, recklessly endanger, or threaten the wife. That was it. That is what we sometimes refer to as a "limited order." The order could also have provided that he was to stay away from her and to vacate the family home. It did not. There was an appeal by the wife. The appellate court, again with a woman judge writing for a four-judge panel in one of the four New York Appellate courts, held that that was an error, that the judge should have ordered the husband out of the house. Obviously, how could you assure this woman's safety with someone who had knocked her unconscious and she is wheelchair-bound? The decision was just that long. It was just one line. And then there was the second line, however, as our intermediate appellate court can make new findings of fact based on the trial record and go beyond the trial court's finding. And so based on the record, they held that the wife had testified that she had slapped the husband and therefore he was also entitled to a protection order against her. I thought that the slap probably sounded to me like a defensive act, but certainly would not threaten him as she was wheelchair-bound, but that was the decision. I thought it was shocking. I was long off the bench by then. I never did have lunch with my colleague. I did not have the opportunity to tell her what I thought of it. I left that to a mutual friend. But it is not easy to change course. Judges have discretion, and that is why good lawyering and making a record is the answer to making a difference in the court.

One of the reasons our divorce courts are different from our family courts in New York is because the lawyers come into the divorce court with a different kind of advocacy, along with the kind of money they can spend on building their cases with evidence because divorces are fought about money. Custody is often a surrogate for the real issue of money. "If I get custody, I do not have to pay child support, do I? If I get custody, I probably will not have to pay spousal support because I can say if I do, it is only for a limited time because that spouse without children to care for can go to work." So there are motivations other than love of children for fighting custody.

Another issue is one of continued power and control by the domestic violence offender. He controls the life of his wife by bringing the children back late, coming to pick them up early, fighting over which days he is going to have them, when it is going to be changed, why it is going to be changed, having to go out of town on a business trip and not take the children on a day when she expected them to be with their father and she planned a business meeting or a job interview. So her life is completely controlled by the custody and visitation schedule. But you have judicial discretion, and there is a limit to what you can do because judges have that power, and that is our job, to use our discretion to make hard decisions, and follow the law in addition.

So we get to the issue of the mental health evaluations. When I came to the family court, I was told, "We have to have a mental health evaluation in this case, Judge." "Why?" "Because it's a child in this case." "Okay. Why do we need a mental health evaluation? Child abuse is an issue of fact. Why do I need an expert witness on mental health for that? Is somebody supposed to be mentally ill or have a mental disorder here?" "No, but in all the child abuse cases, judges order mental health evaluations." So I did. I then learned that when you get a bad mental health evaluation, not in its outcome, but in its substance in that there are inconsistencies in the evaluation and the report, where the conclusion is inconsistent with the comments made before, I had to spend my weekend writing a decision explaining why I found the report unpersuasive and why I was going to ignore everything in it, from the first line to the last. I said, "Never again." In 16 years on the bench, I only ordered mental health evaluations when there was an issue either in the pleadings (in the petition or the complaint) that raised the issue of somebody's mental health; i.e., this person should not have custody of these children because she is suicidal. Okay. That needs an evaluation. If there is an issue of a child's special needs and the parents' capacity to meet them, the child is mentally disturbed, the child has serious emotional problems that need a parent who is particularly attuned and the other parent doesn't deal with it, maybe I want an evaluation of the child to determine what those needs are. But I have to evaluate that parent in the courtroom, listening to the testimony to determine whether that parent understands the child's needs, knows how they need to be dealt with, and the other is whether that parent has empathy.

Now, I know we cannot measure empathy, but you sure know it when it is absent. And you know it when you see it. When no one calls, as a witness, the father who has just been released from prison for having battered his child, causing brain damage, comes to court seeking return of the child from foster care to his custody because he has paid his debt to society, fulfilling his prison term and now he's entitled to have his child back and nobody calls him as a witness, the judge did. Let's hear about it. Tell me about your child. Does he have any special needs? What are they? How would you deal with them? He says, "There is nothing wrong with him. All he needs is his father." So we have the medical records. We know the child had brain damage, and the child was with a foster parent who really dealt with these issues, had made a decision to take this injured child into her care, and was doing a wonderful job by everybody's estimate. In New York, every child has a lawyer, not a guardian *ad litem*, but a lawyer who is the child's lawyer. The Legal Aid Society in New York has a juvenile rights division that has investigators. Their investigator went to the home, met her, and observed her. They all hired a psychologist to do an observation and a social worker who testify as to whatever we need. In one instance, they sent their social worker out of state to observe the children in their home with their mother and to ask the children about their father. The children never came to court, and the social worker got on the witness stand and testified that the child said that "every night I went to bed terrified of going to sleep because I thought Daddy was going to kill Mommy," and he heard the violence going on in the next room, and this was the testimony. Of course the father said it never happened and he was just this wonderful guy. He did not get visits.

But these are issues, how they come out and how you decide them if you are balanced. If you give him contact anyway, you are denying the children their remedies; you are denying the mother her remedy and her safety. If we defer to mental health professionals, I think we are doing something we are not allowed to do, and that is the unconstitutional delegation of our adjudicatory responsibility. We have to adjudicate the case, not the mental health professional. That is one piece of evidence. It can be persuasive. It can be useless. But we have to decide it. And by not having the mental health professional, we save not only money for the litigants and the court system and time, the months it takes to do the evaluation, write the report, review it, and then present it. We save all that. And we also save an irrelevant, tangential issue. The report takes on a life of its own. Is it valid? Is it good? The examination of the maker, the maker's qualifications. What are your qualifications to make this report? What scholarly literature do you use on which you rely in making reports? That becomes this tangential issue that absorbs all the time.

The real issue is: Who are these parents? I always like to hear the parents testify. I like to watch the other parent listening to the opposing parent testify. It will be very informative. What is your case? You have an argument. A lawyer's argument is not persuasive—forgive me—but evidence is persuasive. Lawyers will say anything. Right? They have to. They are paid to. You know, alienation, child sexual abuse, they expect the judge to leap off the bench and embrace them, give them the courthouse when they just allege these things. Fine. You have made this allegation; I'll hear your evidence. Show me. And five years of child abuse cases in the Bronx, with a docket that never had less than 50 cases a day, I'd seen a lot of child abuse and heard a lot of excellent expert testimony from some of the best people I think of in the field. There is a team at Bellevue Hospital with a pediatrician, Margaret McHugh, and two psychologists. Dr. McHugh does the child examination and talks to the child, does some very creative interaction with children. Then the psychologists each interview the child. Each psychologist writes her report without the conclusion. They exchange their raw data and then they meet to discuss it to see if they both come out with the same result. So it is fascinating. It is really good evidence, and when I once called Dr. McHugh as my witness and the respondent's lawyer said, "Oh, you can't do this; this is terrible. How can you do this? If you do this, you are going to believe her" and, you know, my client. I said, "I have no idea what she is going to testify, and you will be able to examine her." She exonerated his client. I do not remember if he thanked me, but she did. Part of it was, I was suspicious, and the first doctor was not convincing to me. And I looked at his slides and I did not see anything wrong. I think he just did not know what a three-year-old vagina should look like. He was not a pediatrician.

So making the decision is the judge's job. But we cannot stop judges from having mental health evaluations. There is no way you can do it. It is within the judge's discretion to decide that. So just writing statutes does not always work. You know, you can say you cannot give the abuser custody and then the judge says, "I find that there was no abuse sufficient to harm this child."

And resilience is the other. You know, oh, the child is not affected by the domestic violence; he's doing very well in school. I do not have to tell the psychologist what that means. It could very well be where the child is retreating to his zone of safety and getting some mastery in his life to overcome the trauma of what he is suffering at home.

I am not going to spend time on parental alienation except to say what you all know. It is not a syndrome. It is not admissible in my state. It is not admissible in many states. It is the result of the self-published work of someone who had no empirical data, and we have heard all of that and we know that, never a peer review published in a psychological journal. And it is now the subject of a vast public relations machine. We have the celebrity effect, the Hollywood stars involved, and it has infiltrated our courts, and it will not go away. And one of the ways it has infiltrated now is: it has taken on a new life. It is not a syndrome anymore. It is just the fact of alienation and it's common. No, it's not. How many custody cases have we done? The mere allegation of it may never go anywhere, so that is one category. But the number of parental alienation cases that have a life sufficient that they go to trial is infinitesimal. I would love to see a docket study, and this would be a wonderful thing to do. How many cases is custody pleaded? Or how many custody petitions with nothing else are filed? So you could have divorce cases where there is a custody issue or where there isn't and there is only a money issue. Then, how many of those cases are settled before trial? About 90%. But I would like to see hard numbers. If they weren't, we would still be sitting 24/7 in the way we do criminal arraignments in New York City, where we had three judges around the clock because everyone has to be out within 24 hours before a judge. I sat criminal arraignments on a Thanksgiving Day. I did 200 arraignments. I wasn't the best because I wasn't pushing the files down the chute fast enough, and the officer came over and told me that, so I got better. It was so awful; it was the only courtroom I had ever been in where they did not have water for the judge on the bench. They did not tell me before I went that I had to bring my own bottle of water to the courtroom. And I won't tell you how filthy the robing room was. It was so dusty that I spread out the sports section of the *New York Times* to sit on so I wouldn't get dust on my robe.

So we would have to do that in custody cases if every custody case were tried. It is nowhere near that. They are settled. The few that are tried do not take that long. Most of the time it is one party that testifies, unless you get the evaluation, which can be a long examination, with qualification of the witnesses and the expert, then raising the standards on which this expert is testifying. How do we reach the Daubert standard of what is well accepted in the scientific community, which we know parental alienation syndrome does not. So you have that. And what is the response that we get? Yeah, we're settling custody cases, most of them, because they are not real custody cases. But I would like to see hard numbers. I think it would be wonderful.

And the other is: What is the court system's response to too many domestic violence cases? And there are a lot. And one of the reasons is, there are remedies in law now that were not there 40 years ago in most states, and they are being used. So as that information spreads, victims come to court to seek the legal remedies. And the court system says, what do we do about this? We defer these and we divert these cases to mediation, and that is in my article that is available outside at the front desk. And why is mediation bad in these cases? Well, one is, there is a power imbalance, and the mediation module—and some of you, I assume, may be mediators—is that you have got the independent, voluntary, private decision-making by two individuals. If one of them has all the power and the other one does not, you are not going to get a fair outcome, because one party's independent decision-making is overborne by the other one's power. I once said to a friend, "What does the battered woman give up? Child support? The house? No. Spouse maintenance? What does she have with which she can negotiate? She cannot negotiate with the lives of her children. So mediation is terrible in domestic violence cases, by my perception of it.

The other is that the goal in mediation is an agreement. The content of that agreement is irrelevant. It is the outcome of an agreement. That is a positive. So when you have mediation programs, you calculate their effectiveness by the number of successful mediations, and that means agreements. Not the content, just the agreement. Mediation looks to the future. We only want to deal with future conduct. Therefore, there is no accountability for your past behavior. One of the theories that the domestic violence movement has taught is that domestic violence offenders have to be held accountable. Well, there is no accountability in mediation because we do not discuss what you did before you walked into this room for the mediation. We want a solution. There is no protection order. There is an agreement for future relations between two people, one of whom holds all the cards, the other of whom has hope and nothing else. My clients usually came to me after five years of domestic violence. They had tried everything. They had gone to their priests. They had gone to their doctors. The families had intervened. There was informal mediation that had gone on. If it had worked, they would not have needed a divorce and they would not have had to come to court. People do not go to court when they have an option. If mediation worked, then domestic violence would have declined. It didn't. It didn't until we began to have arrests, prosecutions, protection orders, and of course shelters.

There are no empirical data that established the efficacy of mediations to stop family violence. None. And yet the court systems are using it more extensively as a way to deal with the lack of funding, the inability to add more judges—which we have been trying to do in New York, I think, for at least 20 years now. They will not add one more family court judge. But there is a wonderful political problem involved, you see. And that is, do we have judges by county or by judicial districts?—Which would be like legislative districts. Well, in one, you get more Republican judges; in the other, you get more Democratic judges. And since the Senate is Republican and the Assembly is Democratic, we have never gotten an additional family court judge in 20 years. And, you know, if anybody is looking for a really important reason, that is the only reason.

The data from the Bureau of Justice Statistics are amazing. I had not looked at them in years, and I was working in Japan in 2003 and writing lots of papers at their request. I said, "I need to go and look at the Bureau of Justice Statistics latest data," and there is a chart and it has the data from 1976 to 2003. In the chart regarding intimate partner homicides, the female line is level and then it declines a little. The male intimate partner homicides show an incredible dip. In my looking at it, it was like somebody kicked me in the gut. I could not believe this. That was all of the statutory changes, the changes in government policy, police, and prosecutors. Men were surviving, and it was a 71% decline in the men murdered by their intimates as of 2002. The decline for women was 23%. And what that meant was that women, given an option, were escaping and not killing the offenders. They went to the shelters. They got divorced. They had an option. But men were still killing the women they had been beating for years. And it has not changed. In fact, we have a slight uptick in the number of white women being killed by their intimate partners. I might say that the decline of 71% is consistent for white men, African-American men, and African-American women. And when you look at the patterns of response from the Bureau of Justice Statistics, the bias that African-American women would not call the police because the police are the enemy in the community is incorrect. African-American women are saving their lives by calling the police. They are most likely to call the police. White women are not as likely to call the police.

And then of course the most dangerous time is post-separation, and there is a 41% increase in violence. That is nonfatal violence. But the most dangerous time for a woman is when she is separated from her intimate partner, and there is a 41% increase in the violence. You will be pleased to know that married women have a lower level than that. Divorced women have a higher level than married women. Widowed have infinitesimal violence from their intimate partners, which is good, because at least we know that death ends this. And never married have a small amount also.

But the shock for me was to see that all the work was really not saving women's lives the way they should be. At the same time that the intimate-partner homicides against women had decreased 23%, the aggregate homicide rate in the U.S. had declined by 30%. So women with intimate partners were not even keeping pace with the general homicide decline in the U.S. I am almost done; I think you'll be happy.

I have some recommendations, and I thought that would be a good idea, and hopefully you will have time to grill me on all this, and you have been taking notes about questions you are going to ask.

One is, forget family court if you can, and go right through the divorce. Now, in New York you can get your protection order with your divorce. No reason not to, because the divorce is in the Court of General Jurisdiction. It can do anything and everything by our constitution that the family court can do, that the Surrogates Court can do. Those are two equal courts. But the Supreme Court, as we call it when everywhere else it is Superior Court, has all the jurisdiction, and there is no reason to do it in two steps. And if you lose that family court protection order proceeding, you then have a heavier burden in the divorce court. But you also are going to be faced with something that Laura Dugan and her colleagues found years ago: When there is a weak response, the police arrive and say, "If you're married, there is nothing we can do" and walk out. The prosecutor will not prosecute. What happens is: you get a retaliation effect from a weak response, not from a robust response. So if you lose that protection order proceeding, your life is at greater risk. You are likely to be assaulted, especially if you are separated, and you are going to increase it that much more. You do not want to lose. Knowing what the dockets are like in the family court, knowing your bench, and deciding whether or not it is safe to go there, you are better off just getting the divorce. In no-fault divorce, you do not have to prove anything other than irreconcilable differences. And irreconcilable differences is a subjective standard within the person petitioning, although some of our judges faced with it for the first time thought they needed a hearing about this. I think the appellate court straightened them out. The whole purpose of no-fault divorce is not to try the cause of action. You do not need to. There isn't one.

Not using mental health evaluations, and not requesting them, because sometimes the lawyers do that as a maneuver to raise the cost and thus litigate the other party into poverty. The judge can say, "No, thank you." That is judicial discretion. Lawyers make requests. Judges dispose of them. "Yes" or "no," like when I had laryngitis and I sat and I could not even croak and I had to rule on objections, and my court reporter said, "I never felt more powerful." And she was as she stated, "the Judge said." She had a grand time while I was miserable.

The other problem that comes up with mental health evaluations is one that is, I think, easily resolved, and that is substance abuse. Mental health evaluations, in my view, are useless in substance-abuse evaluations. Why? Because the person allegedly abusing substances is going to fill that report with self-serving denials. "No, I didn't." "If I ever did, I stopped." You know, it is like the kids: "I found the gun under the car on my way to school, and I was going to take it to the police after school." That is why he had a gun in school. "I was just holding it for my friend" or my favorite, "My client is going to plead guilty," and we have what we call an allocution, and you have to tell the judge what you did wrong. And there are some judges who will allow reading the charge and say, "Did you do it?" and somebody nods or says, "Yes," and that's okay. And I was not satisfied, so, "Tell me what you did wrong." The response, "I got arrested."

The other is not to use evaluations in substance abuse. Surprise lab tests are the gold standard. Somebody calls, "Go to the lab now." If you don't go, the judge draws a negative inference: What are you hiding? You are not cooperating. The test is conclusive. It is like the test for mental retardation: It either is or it isn't. There is no maybe. And that saves time and money, and you have objective test results from the lab without all the manipulation by the substance abuser or the person who is honestly defending himself or herself, saying, "I don't abuse anything. I'm not a drinker and I don't take drugs."

The other important thing for evaluators to remember is that the prior court determinations are conclusive. If there is a judgment, a finding by a court, be it a family court, a divorce court, or a criminal court, if somebody committed an offense against a spouse, then that is a given fact from which your evaluation flows. No matter what kind of charming denials you get, no matter how much you like the offender more than the former victim, no matter how appealing he is, your evaluation cannot be vague about whether or not it happens. It cannot say the father or the mother denies this happened. It's a fact. When you say that, you can say, "And therefore I find this person an unreliable informant." He was not forthcoming. But that is the given. And if the report does not have the documents or does not say, "I looked for them and could not finding any," does not say that the lawyer for each party and the court clerk—"What are all the prior files? May I have a print-out of the docket" or goes into the court system record and gets the printout to know what to look for, these are indispensable collateral to your evaluation. Without that, I don't care who you interview, you know that his mother is going to say he's wonderful. But if the criminal was found beyond a reasonable doubt that he committed a misdemeanor assault, there is no discussion here. That's the end of it. The Saunders study is excellent and I really commend it to you. It is just wonderful, because they looked at every element, and they did wonderful interviews. They had a large sample. It is really methodologically compelling.

The other is that a way to defuse custody fights in domestic violence or nondomestic violence cases is to impress upon your client that it is the child's right to have contact with the parents when it is safe. It is not the right of the mother. It is not the right of the father. It is the child's right. And then you see as I have seen people actually relax when they realize they were not fighting for their rights anymore, but it was the right of the child to have contact when it is safe. They are usually okay with that. In a lot of cases in family court, people do not have lawyers. It is a poor-person's court. And you are talking to litigants without being filtered by lawyers.

Okay. And we need mental health evaluations when we have mental illnesses or mental disorders because we need a diagnosis.

There was a defendant father in a divorce case who had a law degree from a very fancy law school. I do not remember which one it was, but, believe me, I could not afford to go there. I think it was Harvard. He then said that he had worked for this law firm and that law firm, and he had gotten fired by two of the major fancy law firms in New York. And you really have to do bad things to get fired. He had not worked in ten years at any job. He had violated the prior judge on the case. I was the backup trial judge, so I got the case if the other judge who had it hated it or hated the lawyers. That was the standard, you know, in judicial discretion. They would transfer the case to me, and I caught all the junk cases. And sometimes, you know, you could see why the judge hated the lawyers and sometimes the parties, and other times, you know, it was a lot of work so I got it. And this man had violated a prior order to bring the child back at 7 o'clock, and his reason was: it did not say "Eastern Standard Time." We are dealing with a person who has, you know, some thought disorders, a little reality-testing problem here, and this social worker, who was appointed by the prior judge, got on the stand to testify and was talking about the parent-child interaction with the two parents, and she went on and on as they examined her. I was not hearing anything about his obvious mental disturbance. He is probably psychotic. I said, "And did you reach a diagnosis?" And she said, "Oh, no, we never do diagnosis in a custody evaluation." Not even if it comes up and punches you in the face? So it was all useless as I needed a diagnosis if I was going to do anything. Ultimately, I terminated all his contact when he showed up in violation of an order of protection, hiding behind a bookcase in the child's day-care center, terrifying absolutely everybody, and then was stalking the childcare person in the park who was with this child. They issued a warrant for his arrest for violating the order of protection, and the New York City Police Department would not honor my arrest warrant because I was sitting civil term and not criminal term. Luckily, I knew the Chief of Police in Nassau County where the family lived, and he was going to enforce my order, but they could not find him. They actually searched for him and they could not find him. I could not get the police department to talk to me, maybe because we sued them in 1976 even though they settled. But, you know, nobody there was old enough to remember that they settled. But we had settled that case and they agreed to mandatory arrest before the legislatures began enacting mandatory arrest statutes, which was in 1994 when it just kind of took off all across the U.S. But the New York State legislature waited until 1994. But in New York City, we had this judgment consent against the police that they had to have mandatory arrests.

By the way, we did not sue the court. We sued the Chief Clerk of the Court. You cannot sue a judge. Judges have immunity from suit. You cannot sue a judge for what the judge does in the courtroom. You can arrest a judge for drunk driving. You can arrest a judge for assault. But you cannot sue a judge based on a decision. You can make an appeal. And if you win, that is the best judicial education, because judges never do that again when they get reversed. The appellate courts give great deference in custody cases to the trial judge because the trial judge had the unique opportunity to observe the witnesses and listen to their testimony, and the appeal court gets a written transcript, but you saw that family and your decision is given great deference.

It is very hard to get a reversal on a custody case. My favorite is the one in which the trial judge said the father and his second wife would be much better custodial parents than the mother, giving the child a stable two-parent household. The only problem was, as the appellate court found, there was nothing in the record to indicate that the father had a second wife or even was planning to have a second wife. She didn't exist except in the judge's mind because he thought that this man would have good judgment and his second wife would be good; he only made a mistake with the first one. So that was a reversal, but it is one of the rare ones. Or the one in which the judge delegated to the mental health professional the future determination of the amount of contact between the father and the child. This evaluator was going to determine when the visits could be unsupervised and how the visits would be, and the appellate court said that is inappropriate delegation of the judicial responsibility to this mental health professional, and that was reversed. These are interesting, but they were rare.

The gender bias commissions convened in the 1990s found that gender bias exists in almost every state. Most federal judicial districts also had them. They studied gender bias in the courts. They had hearings. They had focus groups. They did surveys and interviews. We did it in New York. We did it all over the country. And overwhelmingly the courts found that there was systemic bias against women in all the courts.

When I started with the New York Gender Bias Commission, I remember the senior lawyers from very prominent law firms who had been appointed by the governor to the commission, and they said there was no such thing. "It just does not happen. I can't imagine this happening." They were men of goodwill and they did not practice any bias that they were aware of. By the end of two years, they were completely converted. They were carrying the torch to end gender bias in the courts.

One of the responses that the courts thought would be good was to mandate gender-neutral language, and they published a little gender-neutral language guide, and all that we have is bias hidden by gender-neutral language. It does not change the way you think on fundamental issues. It changes the interaction. And it also leads to some interesting use of terminology such as "the pregnant person." Yeah, and that's when you know the gender-neutral language is not a good idea. It hides the gendered nature of violence against women, which the Violence Against Women Act addresses, which European countries see as a human rights violation, which the Inter-American Commission on Human Rights found the United States to have violated the human rights of Jessica Lenahan in Colorado when the police refused to enforce the protection order for her three children and they died. I am unclear whether their father had killed them or the hail of police bullets that were discharged at the father when he drove up with his pickup truck at 5 o'clock in the morning to the police station and opened fire on the police; they returned the fire. No autopsy results were ever done. Nobody knows whose bullets killed those children. And that is one of the bases for the Inter-American Commission finding of human rights violation against the United States. The United States Supreme Court held that the police failure to enforce the order of protection, failure to arrest or even pursue the father who had the children in violation of the court order and in violation of the Colorado statute that gave the police the responsibility of mandatory arrest for violating a protection order was not a violation of the statute.

Now, I do not know when "must" and "shall" are not mandatory and "mandatory" isn't, but the Supreme Court held it wasn't. It is a very interesting decision. It is Castle Rock v. Gonzales. It is the City of Castle Rock. Since between that decision and the hearing in the Inter-American Commission on Human Rights, Jessica Gonzales married again and her name is now Lenahan. So that is—Lenahan v. The U.S. But that is an interesting decision, which I could not imagine writing myself.

The legislative intent has an impact on what judges write in their decisions and how they apply the law, and judges should not ignore the responsibility of providing protection orders to victims who have proven the domestic violence. I am not saying everybody who walks in the courtroom and alleges something is telling me the truth. I am a recovering judge. I am skeptical. I always was. And once you are a judge, you are always a recovering judge, and skepticism is there. You know, somebody comes in and says, "I want you to represent me" and "This terrible thing happened, a miscarriage of justice," ra-ra-ra. I said, "I'll read the transcript and then we'll talk." It is not in my pecuniary interests. I may lose a client. But that is okay. I am not going to stand up in a courtroom and make an argument and fail the red-face test.

When you look at the legislative intent, the New York Court of Appeals, which is our highest court—called "Supreme Court" in every other state except New York—we are unique. We have nine different kinds of trial courts. A lot of sitting judges do not know what all the other courts are. It is not worth the effort of learning. But they went into the legislative history and described it and said the purpose of the protection order is to protect the victim of domestic violence. And prior to 1981, the statute had a provision which said that the purpose of a protection order was to keep families together, and the legislature repealed that, because the purpose is not to keep families together. The purpose is to provide safety and stop violence in the family.

I have two articles in the front desk outside. One is the diversion from courts article in which I have some of the BJS data, the Bureau of Justice Statistics data, and the other one is an article I published in the United Kingdom, which is on bias against women witnesses, which is consistent with Saunders, et al.'s finding that there is bias against women. We do not believe women when they say they are victims of domestic violence. We generally do not give as much credibility to women witnesses as we give to men. And it is not just male justices. I mean, women judges, particularly younger ones, who will say things like, "I never experienced any discrimination," and of course I know that because we took care of that. Right? So they had no discrimination. They were more than 50% of their law school classes. They were not one woman among the whole sea of men in law school. Their professor did not make funny comments, because he knew he was outnumbered. And you have really no change in that. And what I looked at is some of the historic data that establishes it, such as in rape cases, where in the 1950s they were always called "alleged" rape victims—right? We always called them "alleged" but we don't have "alleged" bank robbers, do we? We don't have "alleged" bank presidents who have been robbed. We only have alleged rape victims. Women who are accusing someone of rape should take lie-detector tests. For no other criminal complaint was that ever an issue. It never came up. But it was recommended or urged. Also, there is the work of Lee Beenan, who was a public defender in New Jersey, who is also a published poet and is now teaching in Chicago. She did a series of analyses of rape laws in the 1970s. She also looked at how rape victims were treated. *Wigmore on Evidence,* which is the evidence treatise, big volumes of books, in which I had a section in which it talked about women and girls lying and fantasizing about rape. One of the bases for this was a study of nine little girls who were claiming to have been sexually assaulted. Beenan went back and looked at the history, and these were nine little girls who were in a psychiatric hospital. So that was then extrapolated to all women and girls who cannot be trusted.

In England a couple of years ago, there was a mass rapist loose, and the women were going to the police in great numbers, and the police were not taking note. They were not writing it up as a crime. Why? Because the women said they were drunk. That was the M.O., modus operandi or method that this rapist used. He got them drunk. He said, "I just won the lottery. I have champagne. Will you celebrate with me?" He would get them drunk, rape them, and drop them on their doorsteps.

A second element in the finding that the police did not find the women credible because they were drunk was the way the police mishandled Worboys, which was the name of the suspect in the case. This was revealed just last month in a major review in why the police found there was no crime. In addition to the notion that the women were not credible because they were drunk, was the fact that Worboys was a guy who drove a black London cab.

These are the people who take the test showing they know every street in London and they know how to get everywhere, even though the streets change their name in midblock when you have not even crossed a highway or a roadway. Many London streets change their name in the middle of a block, such as a street named South End is suddenly Thurlow Square. I have walked this block a hundred times and I never realized that its name changed in the middle. Not only that, the post code changed too. One long block has three post codes.

So he found that the police would not believe that a black cabdriver who had what they called the knowledge, knew the streets and the routes, could be guilty. Or as one comedian said, "they know the shortest route from every point to every other point and they have a million reasons that they cannot take that route." But that was the police bias. So the women were drunk, and it could not be him. So he got away with it for at least another 10 rapes before he was finally arrested. And he was convicted. And there was a second serial rapist also around, and the same problem: the women were not being relied on, and the police were not gathering the data to even see the pattern.

I hope there will be lots of questions later when we get a chance. I have just been given the hook. Thank you.

Chapter 3
Discussion with Dr. Walker and Judge Fields

Lenore E. Walker, Ed.D., A.B.P.P.
and Hon. Marjorie Fields, J.D.
(As transcribed from the recording of the audience's interchange)

DR. JANET CUMMINGS: Instead of having the Reactor Panel that is listed on your schedules, in the interest in staying more or less on time, I am simply going to ask Dr. Walker and Judge Fields to return to the front to entertain questions. If you do want to ask a question or make a comment, please use the microphone so that you will be on that all-important recording.

MALE SPEAKER from the AUDIENCE: Shall we start asking questions?

DR. JANET CUMMINGS: Yes, please.

FIRST AUDIENCE SPEAKER: Okay. I have a question for Judge Fields. You mentioned that if a court has already made a finding, then an evaluator should take that finding as fact and go from there, and you were primarily describing positive findings that somebody had done something. But often there are situations where the court had made sort of a lack of finding and had not found that a child had been abused. But this was often based either on poor interpretation of the data or on weak evidence or whatever—inadequate evaluations—so, as an evaluator on occasion, I think it would be inappropriate for me to accept that court's finding or lack of finding because they might be missing something important. So I just wanted to clarify if you were talking only about positive findings that something was done or how you would address this issue?

JUDGE FIELDS: I was definitely talking about positive findings in that context. However, the obverse is a serious problem. If the court has found that there has not been any child abuse proven—and that is by a preponderance of the evidence—you are really stuck with that unless you can come up with new evidence that had not been before the court, which is a possibility. And, in addition, what should happen at that point is, the case should be reopened, because newly discovered evidence that was not available and was not presented to the court can get a changed finding, and that would be part of the responsibility to say, "Look. There's evidence that hadn't been presented here that is medically and psychologically conclusive of the issue or very strong—much stronger than what had been presented." But you are stuck with the finding of no abuse or failure to prove abuse until you have got something to show, and that is new evidence.

There is also what I used to characterize as not new evidence but lately subpoenaed; in other words, what somebody did not bother to marshal and bring into court. That is more difficult as to whether you would reopen in that case. But you are really stuck with the court's determination when you are working in the court.

DR. WALKER: Now, I want to just add to that. I have been in a number of cases where the judge not only has made there is no finding or insufficient finding or insufficient evidence, but that if the mother or anyone reports child abuse again, the mother will lose custody. It will change custody immediately. The child may be a preschooler and tells the teacher that he or she has been abused; the teacher is in the mandatory category of report and has to make the report. Often the judge then claims that the mother has put the child up to it and changes custody in ex parte hearings without having a hearing. And this is happening again and again and again to the children, and I end up working in these cases. What's the remedy?

JUDGE FIELDS: The remedy is an appeal and a stay. That is one possibility. If a judge has at that point changed custody, then the idea is to go to the appellate court, but it is not necessarily going to work. However, if you have got new evidence of child abuse, the appellate court is likely to grant the stay of the change of custody out of concern for the child because this is such a serious allegation. But whether it is going to mean that in the end you are going to prevail with it is different because it has got to go to trial.

Sometimes what the appellate court will do is say this case goes back to trial before a different judge. That's a bad-judge-slap-on-the-wrist decision. But you have no guarantees. It is very difficult. Judicial discretion has got very few limits. It is really a pretty powerful thing. That is why, you know, judges can do a lot of stuff that we disagree with, like the Castle Rock decision in which "shall arrest" was not mandatory and therefore it was okay, and Colorado and Castle Rock were not liable for the death of these three little girls, and the fact that there had not been an autopsy was completely lost. And that is just to save any state from the liability they would have if they found out it was the police bullets that killed these children, that they did not manage to get this guy subdued and find out if the children were in the truck when they started their firing back in self-defense, obviously. They were entitled to defend themselves.

SECOND AUDIENCE SPEAKER: I do not feel very organized, but I am trying to get something across here. Regarding Castle Rock, they got the same decision we got in our child sexual abuse case, where the father was awarded sole custody based on parental alienation. We lost our appeal based on the United States Supreme Court, DeShaney case law, which is based on the United States Constitution, and it was, you know, translated into children do not have a right to be protected from abuse by a parent. It's not worded that way, but that is how it is translated: Children do not have a right to be protected.

JUDGE FIELDS: It works out that way.

SECOND AUDIENCE SPEAKER: Yeah.

JUDGE FIELDS: Look at what happened in Wisconsin; Winnebago County, Wisconsin. But the Child Protective Services had gone to see the child when he was with his father, and the child went back and forth. The father had time with the child, and the child lived with him for some days and then with the mother for the others. When they went, each time the father said the child was asleep. The Child Protective Service workers then left and did nothing else. Ultimately, the child was returned to the mother, suffering severe brain damage from brutal attacks by the father, and the United States Supreme Court said the State of Wisconsin could not be held liable for the failure to investigate. And what that has resulted in is police also not feeling that they couldn't be held liable for failing to respond in domestic violence cases with adults as well.

Now, we have not tried that. But the DeShaney case has ripple effects across the board with regard to police responsibility to investigate. There is no duty to protect the citizen. There is only duty when the government, the police, the state, takes the responsibility. And I may distinguish it for you. When the police say, "We are going to drive by" or "We are going to have a car outside your home and we will keep you safe from having your violent partner break into the home and assault you or shoot you" and they promise they will do this, they are assuming the duty to protect this one citizen. But there is no general duty to protect citizens. So if you call the police and ask for their help and they do not come, there is no liability, because they assumed no responsibility.

It is a very difficult standard and very high one. Every case in New York has held police "no liability" in the last 40 years. When the police arrived, they interviewed the children in front of the father, and they asked, "Are you afraid?" and they said, "Oh, no," with their father standing right there. The police left, and the reason they hadn't been called was that the father had smashed the windshield of the mother's car. He would not let her take the children with her. He had set fire to her clothes in the front yard. He had been threatening and beating her, and she was worried. That night, he murdered his children, set fire to the house, and there was no liability. And that was one of the earliest New York cases, and it just continued, but it was post DeShaney.

So DeShaney gives pretty much carte blanche for police to run their response as they see fit, and there is no duty, even with the mandatory arrest statutes now that we have Castle Rock. So that extended it, and it is not in terms of the child's right. It is in terms of the police responsibility, the Child Protective Services responsibility. Their malpractice is not actionable.

THIRD AUDIENCE SPEAKER: I just want to give you this information: The court found this father sexually abused his son and daughter, including, but not limited to, repeatedly sodomizing and forcing oral copulation. I also want to note the Court Transcript by Judge DeNasio. It was in The Case at Bar. The perceived time was specific, horrific sexual assaults perpetrated many times, skillfully concealed. Now, that was basically in dependency court, the first court finding. The family court awarded the father sole custody based on parental alienation. The mother in the case was sentenced to 12 years in prison, with the family court putting a $25 million bond on her. And she could not appear at her criminal trial because of the $25 million bond.

DR. WALKER: Did she leave the jurisdiction of the court with the children? Or why was she criminally charged?

THIRD AUDIENCE SPEAKER: When Child Protective Services police investigation found the father, I guess they substantiated the evidence of severe ongoing sexual abuse....

DR. WALKER: Yes, but why did the mother get arrested?

THIRD AUDIENCE SPEAKER: The father was put on no contact, and actually the Child Protective Services encouraged the mother to go home, which was California, but the case was in Kane County, Illinois, because the father had a 90-day contract for computer work there. So Illinois took jurisdiction because they were there 90 days when my grandson had a torn bloody rectum which was diagnosed by a pediatrician.

DR. WALKER: I am going to ask you to talk to us later about that—

THIRD AUDIENCE SPEAKER: Okay. Very good.

DR. WALKER: The 12 years, because she left the jurisdiction?

THIRD AUDIENCE SPEAKER: Oh, yes, so she did leave the jurisdiction. She was convicted and sentenced to 12 years in prison.

DR. WALKER: Why 12 years?

THIRD AUDIENCE SPEAKER: It was based on—it was very confusing to us, because she enrolled the children in school.

DR. WALKER: These are extraordinarily difficult cases. I did not mention them in my talk, but I do want to go beyond that case.

There are mothers that do take their children, protective moms, who take their children out of the jurisdiction of the court because that is the only way they feel that they can protect their children. We will see a film about that tomorrow called *No Way Out But One*. The problem is that the FBI has made this one of their high-priority crimes. They have labeled it a crime and have made it a high-priority crime. Every case that I have heard about, the mother is arrested. She—that is why I asked right away, did they take her out of jurisdiction—no matter what the father has done or what the findings are of the courts, if you get that far—which in many of these cases you just are getting threats from the judges—and the mothers are eventually found. Their children are turned immediately over to the offending parent, and the mother is usually prosecuted. Sometimes she does and sometimes she doesn't spend time in custody. It is a shame and it should stop. And it should be something that we really demand that the FBI go do the important stuff and let us work on protecting the children in the family courts. They have better things to do than to go after these people.

On the other hand, we as workers in the court really need to understand that if we encourage a mother to do this, we may be dooming her to criminal sanctions and committing a crime. So we may end up with some liability too. And it is something that I think both evaluators and attorneys need to be very aware of. There used to be what we called an underground railroad, but it didn't get very far. The FBI have far more investigatory powers than we do, and they will find them. They just have. And so that is something that we don't make enough noise about, and I thank you for raising that as an issue.

JUDGE FIELDS: It is a federal statute they are enforcing. It is called "The Federal Parental Kidnapping Act" and it has been on the books for a long time, certainly before I went on the bench in 1986. Congress passed a law to prevent parental kidnapping. And it is used against any parent who takes a child in violation of court orders. So if one parent has custody and the other parent takes the child out of state, anywhere, in violation of the custody order and does not bring the child back, without any abuse allegations, just because "I want to take my kid," it is going to be used. So it is used against fathers and mothers. It is used without any allegations of abuse or neglect, not in the kind of case you have. That is extraordinary and pretty awful. I assume she was tried in federal court?

THIRD AUDIENCE SPEAKER: In state court.

JUDGE FIELDS: She was tried in state court. So they did not introduce dependency finding, which is shocking.

THIRD AUDIENCE SPEAKER: The defense lawyer said it was not relevant to the kidnapping.

JUDGE FIELDS: The defense lawyer said it is not relevant to the kidnapping. It is not a defense to the kidnapping, I know, but bringing it in certainly on sentencing, in terms of mitigation for sentencing, it is admissible. On sentencing, you can add all kinds of things that would not be admissible on the original fact-finding, and the federal sentencing statutes require a probation investigation for sentencing, and all of this should have come in at that stage at the very least to prevent a 25-year sentence. This was not a kidnapping in the real sense.

DR. WALKER: All right, let's talk later about that specific case. But I do want to say, Marjory, these are different, as the cases I have been involved with in state court do not pertain to the federal kidnapping statute. These are state court cases where, although they do have the kidnapping statute invoked initially so that they can get the FBI involved. But then the state takes over the cases. And I have been involved in a number of the cases where the court has not permitted testimony from expert witnesses at these trials. So these are pretty scary cases. But let's move on to some of the other things, because we do not have too much time left.

DR. JANET CUMMINGS: It is officially lunchtime, so those of you who wish to go ahead with the lunch break in order to get the full hour may. We will remain and entertain pending questions, so we may or may not get to eat, ladies.

MS. DIANE POST: My name is Diane Post. I am an attorney and I have been doing this since 1976, and my issue is: We have been doing this and nothing you have said is new. We have been litigating, we have been appealing, we have been writing articles, we have been lobbying, and we have been training. We have been doing all of this stuff for 30-plus years, and nothing has changed.

DR. WALKER: That's right.

MS. DIANE POST: And in some ways, it's gotten worse. When I started practicing, I used to be able to get "no contact," no visitation at all, and they can't get that in Phoenix now today. We now have the Gonzales case from the Inter-American Commission on Human Rights that says America is not meeting its international standards. We have at least three countries that have refused to return women to this country because we are not protecting victims. What is it going to take to change it?

JUDGE FIELDS: My theory is we cannot get old doing this because we are doing the same things we did when we were little kids. Everything you said is true. Every issue I raised, we raised starting in the 1970s. It is not even as good as it was, as we have gone backwards. The reason is that the offenders are organized, have the money, have the psychologists that they are able to pay, and have the public-relations machine that has the whole country believing that they are the victims.

DR. WALKER: Yeah, I think that's part of it. But I think the other part of it is very much political. Take a look at the whole politics of the country. We have gone backwards. I'm sorry. I promised I wasn't going to talk politics in Arizona. But I come from Florida, you know, and we are still driving around in trucks with guns in the back of the trucks. So we are not a heck-of-a-lot better in other parts of the country.

AUDIENCE SPEAKER FOUR: Yes, I just had a quick comment or two, and I really appreciate this conference.

DR. JANET CUMMINGS: What is your name?

MS. KATHLEEN RUSSELL: Oh, my name is Kathleen Russell with the Center for Judicial Excellence. It is really important that this dialogue is going on. I appreciated Judge Fields' comments about Canada and Australia and some of the unintended consequences of having national family law, but I also know, having seen media reports, that there has been a national report—at least one, if not multiple—that have come out in the wake of their decision to mandate shared parenting where they have essentially said: This is a screw-up. This has unintended consequences.

Much of that was triggered by a father who went and threw his child off a bridge in a very high-profile murder, which may have been a murder-suicide. And that also leads to my other question, which is: We have been monitoring advocates around the country, the number of revenge killings and murder-suicides or filicides that are going on as a result of botched family court decisions where batterers and child abusers are being given visitation, and we are seeing—literally on a weekly basis—children are being killed. You have got the Katie Tagle case. You've got the Powell case in Washington just a couple months ago. And then we saw the Seal Beach killings, where innocent civilians were in a hair salon getting gunned down because they were in the line of fire.

So sort of in response to Diane's comment: I mean, how many dead children will it take before we can have a real meaningful conversation about reforming the family court? And I deeply appreciate some of Lenore's comments about really taking on some of the sacred cows of how things must be done in family court, because we have got into the level of reform that we really need to be talking about.

DR. WALKER: I absolutely agree with you, Kathleen. One of my colleagues, Vincent Hackels , who is also a police officer who is on the faculty with me, he and I started a study this year of murder-suicides in south Florida because we really have more murder-suicides that are not globally reported, but we are aware of them. And one of my former students has been head of the homicide investigation task force in Miami Dade County where, when I get back, I am going to be meeting for lunch with the person who is in charge of it in Broward County, Florida. These are two very large counties, and we are going to look at these cases and start publishing this work, because I think that one of the ways you get attention in this country is by getting the media to expose case by case by case. It raises people's attention. But we have got to do them in big lumps, because, as you say, we are getting the exposure now of the Powell case and some of the other cases more locally, but they are still not tying together the domestic violence, the child abuse, and the inability of the broken family court system.

I do not think the system is fixable. I am not sure reform at any level is going to fix this system. I just have a feeling it has got to be blown up and we have got to start all over again. It's like my little grandchildren. We take the Lego set and break it up and say, "Let's retake this in." We are going to have the same pieces. I mean, Diane's right. We have been doing it for 40 years, and the pieces are not going to change. But I think we have got to put them together. Wait until you hear Judge Ginger Lerner-Wren tomorrow, who is running the first mental health court in this country, taking apart the criminal court that has been criminalizing mental illness. She has got some good ideas for us, too, tomorrow and how maybe we can infiltrate and change the family court structure some.

DR. JANET CUMMINGS: Yes.

DR. BOB PHILLIPS: I'm Bob Phillips, a doctor of behavioral health from Eastern New Mexico University in Roswell, New Mexico. Thank you, both, very, very much, and I beg your pardon for delaying your lunch.

Dr. Walker, you had mentioned something intriguing to me. If you could say just a little bit more about this notion about reunification being a default kind of thing and the problems. If you could just say more—a little bit more about that for me, please?

DR. WALKER: There are, as you know, Marjory, certain federal statutes that are really just the kind of introduction to the set of laws that are published by states, and they adopt these federal standards and guidelines, and they have no choice. They must adopt these guidelines, right, or they do not get their funding. And the guidelines say very clearly that keeping the family together is a priority, a state priority, and reunification is priority. And so child protective standards in dependency courts have had to take some of that and make some reversals of that presumption, and so they have passed laws that say—for example, in Florida—you have one year in order to complete your program that are given to parents who are in the dependency court, and if you don't, then the court is permitted to look at termination of parental rights.

But had they not passed that law, they could not have gotten beyond terminating parental rights to let the child be in a better home for the child. And that is also because of the presumption that the biological parent is going to have the best interests of the child at heart, when, in fact, we know many biological parents have their own issues and cannot do it, and we can identify that pretty quickly.

So in dependency court, we really have been working a lot on that. But we do not look at it in family court, and that is what I was criticizing, that that presumption carries over to family court. And part of that is because, although we are talking from large communities, when I worked in small towns, the same judge sits on all the courts, dependency—and I see a judge who wants to say something, so why don't we let you—you may have more information.

JUDGE AYCOCK: I just want to make a comment on that issue, because it is not just the law where all those biases and presumptions come in as well. I mean, I hear from judges all the time who tell us that we know—"we," whoever "we" are—we know that children do better when they have contact with both parents. Therefore, I have a built-in presumption in my head that the abusive dad needs to have the children because they need to have contact with the abusive dad. So it is not even just that it is written into the law in places. It is the bias themselves.

DR. WALKER: That is one of the biases. It is very interesting—those of you who watch television—watch *Harry's Law*. The last episode of *Harry's Law* has had exactly what you are talking about, that presumption of bias, and the judge kicks the lawyer off of the woman's case because she is obviously making up all these threats from the man, and you end up with the.... Well, I won't tell you what you end up with. Watch the show on You-Tube, because it is just what we are talking about. I mean, thank goodness for consultants who know something in helping some of the television producers talk.

JUDGE AYCOCK: Here is my question, though it takes you back to the discussion we had earlier about making findings—so in protection order cases—so we are not in a divorce court; we are just in a protection order court—there is some discussion going on about whether or not requiring judges to make a finding of abuse before issuing a restraining order is a good thing or a bad thing. And it basically boils down to an issue of docket control. If I can do consent orders and my incentive to give to the party is that I won't make a finding of abuse, they then agree, I get a quick order, and it is easier for victims to get their order.

Obviously, the problem becomes that there is now no finding of abuse that could have been used in all future kinds of cases. I know right now, for instance, Texas is looking at amending their law to allow no findings in consent orders. In the state of Nevada, we somehow have three sets of laws. We have the law that is Las Vegas, Clark County; we have the law that is Reno in Washoe County; and then we have the law for the rest of the state, which is only about 5 or—5 to 8% of the population.

But, in Washoe County, their position is that if you do not make a finding, you do not have subject matter jurisdiction, because it requires abuse to get the restraining order. In Clark County, it's, "Oh, my God, if you make us do that, I'll never be able to get through my docket." It is how we do it.

So I would just like you to comment on it. I know there is no probably great answer.

JUDGE FIELDS: But it is fascinating to have the rewritten law in every courtroom. I think that happens everywhere, and that is the magic of judicial discretion. Right? But the consent order in a civil proceeding is always permissible. If somebody consents to an order, that's fine. The New York City Police Department consented to mandatory arrest in 1978 rather than go to trial with us. They did not want the publicity, because every time we held a press conference, you could not fit in the room for the cameras, and they just did not want it. So they settled.

But it is enforceable. And the question is: Is the legislature saying that a consent order, protection order, is not enforceable so that you cannot do a violation proceeding if it is violated? If it were a commercial case, landlord and tenant, contract between two businesspeople, if you had a consent judgment, you can enforce that judgment. You could bring contempt if it required performance. So why should it be different in family law? I would love to see a comparison between those cases and family cases. But a consent order should be enforceable. Someone submitting to the jurisdiction, you can do that. The question is: Is it a knowing waiver of a trial? Is it a knowing consent? Is there representation by counsel? Or are we just looking at speed?

Yeah, I mean, that's the mediation thing: Shove it all over to mediation because that is docket control. It is not a judge. We are not wasting judge time on something unimportant like some woman or kid who might get killed. Why do we care?

The other problem here in the U.S. is that children's rights are not given the amount of weight they are given in other countries. And that is shown in the fact that we are the only country in the world that has not signed the International Convention on the Rights of the Child. There is another country, but it does not have a government, and that is Somalia. So we and Somalia are the only ones. So going to children's rights conferences as an American is an embarrassment. You see, anything you say, they throw back at you, and they say, "You don't have a right to talk about this. U.S. hasn't signed the convention on the rights of the child." We are also—as in the Abbott case two years ago, the United States Supreme Court found that the mother had taken the child illegally out of the country of Colombia, even though she had custody, sole custody judgment from the courts in Colombia, and brought the child to the United States, and the reason it was illegal was that the father had not consented to the child being removed. I have not read the briefs. I cannot imagine that it was briefed adequately on the issue of whether the noncustodial parent's consent was required. The case was Abbott, an American mother brought her child back to Texas. The child was then sent back to Colombia where that child would either be with the noncustodial violent father or in foster care. And this is happening all over. And by the way, the country that would not send a U.S. child back to the U.S. because there was violence against the mother, that's Canada. The only country I know that does that.

But there is the Canada case in which they would not send the child back to the U.S. There are more such cases, but one of them is the Canada case. And, you know, when we are dealing with an international child movement or we are dealing with children interstate, with the Interstate Child Custody Act, and the Federal Parental Kidnapping Act. These are not considered defenses. Child abuse is not a defense to taking your child across the border.

And, further, the other problem is that statutes are not sufficient. In the 1970s and 80s, we changed the statutes everywhere in the United States. We created remedies for victims of domestic violence. We created child abuse protection laws that were better and better. However, we are back where we started, and that is because the offenders are organized now and they have the public relations machine and you have the Hollywood effect of people going and talking about parental alienation—"I was deprived of my child"—it could not be anything you did, by any chance, that makes your child not want to see you? But judges run for reelection. Fathers' rights groups make campaign contributions. The press effect is intimidating for judges who have to run for reelection in that there is this whole popular notion that this parental alienation exists, and still the bias against women and children making allegations of sexual abuse and domestic violence exists. So we have all of these prejudices that exist.

Now, what is commonsense? It is common prejudice. And commonsense says women lie; men don't. Men act in their pecuniary interests; they are rational. Women lie; women are irrational. I learned that at a session on negotiation where a woman lawyer said: Yeah, and all women want is revenge in divorce cases, and men are looking to save their money. So it is bizarre, but it is all around us. And how do we change the basic society's prejudice? We thought laws would make a difference. They are not sufficient to overcome this backlash that we are facing, and we do not have the money.

DR. WALKER: Yeah, and I do think that if you take it to the macro level, you see, when there is no money and when states are going bankrupt and there is no money, it gets taken from everything. And it gets taken from the people who scream the least rather than the ones who scream the loudest. And of course it has been children who have no voice. So they do not get hurt. And the moms who try to give voice to the children end up getting punished for it. So, the children get punished for it. So the financial issues are paramount here, as well as the fact that laws are not enough. That is why I said we could blame each profession if we want to, but it is not enough, just as a good psychological report is helpful, but it is not enough. You know, we really need to get beyond that, and we will only be able to do it when we can persuade the people who are the policymakers in the communities within which we live.

And, you know, it happens one case at a time. Like with you, you know. I did not know that Dr. Nick Cummings was that interested in this issue until he called me, you know. It sometimes has to hit home for it to become an issue. But now that it has, hopefully we are going to get your foundation to get involved with other foundations around the country, because they have money and they have voice as well. So, you know, that is going to be, I think, one of the issues that we really have to look at doing.

I do not know about you all, but I have got to eat.

DR. JANET CUMMINGS: Thank you, Dr. Walker and Judge Fields. We will reconvene at one o'clock to hear Dr. John Caccavale.

Chapter 4

The Ethics of Child Custody Evaluations

John Caccavale, Ph.D., J.D.

DR. JANET CUMMINGS: Our next speaker is Dr. John Caccavale who has both a doctorate in psychology and a law degree, and as such is well qualified to address the topic of psychological evaluations in the family court system. As Executive Director of the National Association of Professional Psychology Providers, he represents our co-sponsor for this conference.

I would be remiss if I did not mention that Dr. Caccavale is the 2011 recipient of the Cummings *PSYCHE* Award with its $50,000 prize, psychology's highest award. He was so recognized for his bold, cutting-edge efforts to restore psychotherapy as the first line intervention in behavioral health care. With the same passion, he has joined our effort to reform the family court system. Please welcome Dr. John Caccavale.

DR. JOHN CACCAVALE: Thank you, Janet. I am going to keep this presentation down to 30 minutes. The conflict between business and professional ethics that Dr. Walker referred to is not simply one profession or one group, for when a system is broken as what we have here, you cannot point to just one group or one profession. However, being a psychologist, I believe it is our responsibility to at least look at what we can do with our profession.

Divorce has become a common occurrence in American society. About one in two marriages terminates in divorce. Divorce affects about a million children per year with 10% of divorces involving custody litigation. Child custody evaluations, while initially designed to provide family court judges with unbiased information and data with respect to custody related issues, has become a major profit center for mental health evaluators. Under the guise of "unbiased" assessment, there appears to be a significant departure from real ethical practice. Psychological and psychiatric evaluators have become part of an expansive business enterprise where the interests of children many times is secondary to "How much can I get for this eval?"

This is not to suggest that all evaluators are money hungry, hired guns, or that professionals should not be appropriately reimbursed for their labor. I am suggesting, however, that custody evaluations, in particular, have become a major profit center for many mental professionals who render decisions and recommendations that are not based on any real objective data. Although professional societies develop and publish whole sets of ethical standards, the basis of ethical practice must rest upon the commitment that one does not go beyond what we really know to be true and beyond that what our data can realistically support. This presentation focuses on how professional ethics have become subservient to business interests and to a major contributor to the broken family court system. Some possible solutions also are presented for consideration.

The Foundational Models of Custody Evaluations.

For most of the twentieth century, family courts held to a model whereby the interests of young children in divorce or separation would best be served in the custody of their mothers. This model was based on the recognition that there is a strong maternal bond between mother and child and, moreover, a recognition that mothers nurture children in ways differently than fathers. Added to this was the recognition that mothers, for the most part, were not the main family provider and needed to be home with their children.

During the late 1960s and early 70s, the equal rights movement managed to gain acceptance in custody litigation. Laws were changed to reflect a growing societal goal that both men and women be treated equally. The presumption that mothers be given primary custody over fathers was seen as discriminatory and legally unsupportable. It should be noted that the changes in the law was essentially the product of a political process and not based on the best developmental, psychological, sociological, and rational evidence. Moreover, although many groups supported the change in the model, children and women post-divorce typically now fare economically worse than the male parent. Given the way things have gone from then to now, I am not sure that it is in the best interest of a child when forced to litigate joint custody arrangements.

The result of this change in attitude resulted in a new model for determining custody, but also had the effect of spawning a new industry of custody evaluations and litigation [1]. The present model rests upon the notion that custody should be in the "best interests of the child." This is the legal standard for custody recommendations and decisions in all jurisdictions. Clearly, such a standard is open to wide variations in interpretation and application. This is why custody evaluations have become the norm in custody litigation. The questions remain, however, is on what basis do evaluators rely upon when making recommendations that will affect everyone involved in the process? Should not these recommendations adhere to the highest standards that can reasonably be inferred from all the data underlying the evaluation? Obviously, everyone would agree that they should, but do they really?

Ethical Guidelines For Psychologists In Custody Evaluations.

Although I am concerned about the ethical practice of psychologists in custody evaluations, I am not dismissing any other mental health professionals from my concerns.

Personally, I am dismayed and disappointed in all the professions, including attorneys, who have turned a traumatic event for most parents and children into an adversarial process where the only winners are the bank accounts of those professionals involved in the process. For example, the below graphic of an ad can be seen in almost any newspaper in every city. In all my years of practice, I have never seen an ad that was oriented towards mothers.

What this type of ad typically fosters is a process where mental health professionals and attorneys combine to literally use the legal system to help men use custody as a wedge to gain both economic advantage and freedom from responsibility in divorce. True, there are cases where fathers have been wrongly accused by an angry wife and in those cases men need to have representation. These cases are almost always transparent and do not succeed. Attorneys are professionals who provide services to both sides and cannot be faulted for representing fathers. While we accept that everyone has the right to representation, I contend that the litigation that is so common in custody cases is detrimental and defeats the standard that custody decisions be in the best interests of the child. The interests, as the above ad clearly implies, is for the father. In my opinion, any mental health professional who works with these groups are violating the most important ethical guidelines to function as an impartial evaluator and that the welfare of the child or children is paramount and the focus of the evaluation.

Following are some of the more salient ethical guidelines used by members of the American Psychological Association and provide good illustrations of why ethical guidelines are essentially meaningless and easy to get around for evaluators desiring to put business interests ahead of ethical restraints. All of the guidelines cited can be found on the website of the American Psychological Association [2]. It should be noted that many of the ethical guidelines applied to custody evaluations may be in conflict with ethical guidelines developed for services in other areas of practice.

Guidelines

Psychologists strive to base their recommendations, if any, upon the psychological best interests of the child.

An evaluation with a preconceived notion that a child's interest is best served when equally shared by a mother and a father begins with a bias. Let's face a glaring truth, for most divorces one or both of the parents are so involved with their own issues, the best interest of the child is much lower a priority than personal issues. The myth of the "friendly divorce," albeit a great goal, is rare and there always are some areas of conflict. And, what about the child's choice? While it is typical to get input from an older child in a custody evaluation, it would seem that a child's input should also be a significant factor in deciding custody. There is a wide array of developmental research demonstrating that children in a mother's custody fare much better than when in a father's custody. However, it is not uncommon for evaluators to misquote important research to fit results into the preconceived notion that joint custody is in the best interest of the child.

Case in point: Is joint custody in the best interests of the child? Apparently, the APA believes that it is and that belief, albeit not borne out by all the available research, essentially forms the basis for ethical practice for psychologists who do custody evaluations. For example, a study by Braver, Ellman &. Fabricius [3], has repeatedly been cited by custody evaluators recommending that it is not in the best interest of the child to award primary custody to a divorced mother who desired to move to another state. Braver was so precise in his warning that courts should not allow a parent to move stating: "Moving as little as an hour's drive away from the other parent was a critical issue in their (the child's) mental health and attitudes."

The problem, however, is that the data from this study simply do not support the findings and recommendations that the authors say it does. Among the many findings that the data does support are the following:

1. The most well-adjusted group in this category were children who remained with their mothers.
2. Children in the custody of their fathers scored lowest on general life satisfaction.
3. Children of divorce whose fathers moved away and left them with their mothers were the most satisfied.

This type of misrepresentation is not isolated or rare. There are astute attorneys who know the limitations of research and can correct misrepresentations. However, others are not that astute and few judges are able to sort out the complexities of research design, statistics, and findings that can obscure a wrong interpretation. Moreover, when issues focus on complexities of research design, other issues become lost.

Psychologists strive to avoid conflicts of interest and multiple relationships in conducting evaluations.

Collecting a large fee is perhaps the most significant conflict of interest. Moreover, I know of no evaluator who isn't mindful of future referrals and the need to build and maintain a forensic practice. I am not suggesting that economic motivation always leads to unethical practice. I am suggesting that in every custody evaluation there exists a prime conflict of interest and multiple relationships that can shade recommendations.

The evaluation focuses upon parenting attributes, the child's psychological needs, and the resulting fit.

This guideline essentially opens the door to the notion that the child's best interest is served essentially by putting harm in a hierarchical context from least harm to most harm. The biggest problem is that it allows evaluators to use personality attributes of one or both parents that may have no objective relationship to custody. Moreover, while there are many inappropriate behaviors that parents engage in when in divorce, mental health professionals should not engage in unaccepted, unproven diagnoses or use assessment instruments that cannot possibly be used for the purposes of making a custody evaluation, which is very different from a clinical evaluation.

One problem that is most common in custody cases is a request by either a judge or attorney for one of the parties to offer a custody recommendation from a mental health professional that either was treating the child or one or both of the parents. Besides the many conflicts involved in a provider giving such a recommendation, providers should educate the court that it is not an appropriate request and the reasons why it is not. Whatever takes place in a therapeutic settings may have little to do with which parent deserves custody.

Psychologists create and maintain professional records in accordance with ethical and legal obligations.

One problem with this is that many evaluators refuse to hand over the underlying or raw data to the opposing side. Many times they cite another APA guideline that states that psychologists must maintain the security and integrity of testing materials. Although this is legally unacceptable, I have been involved in many cases where this has been cited. Holding back data, in my opinion, is unethical irrespective of the evaluator's motives.

Psychologists strive to employ multiple methods of data gathering and strive to interpret assessment data in a manner consistent with the context of the evaluation.

This actually combines two separate APA guidelines, but I think that considering them together makes more sense. Data gathered from interview, observation, and traditional testing are different, but all lead to interpretation. This is one area where I believe the greatest occurrence of unethical behaviors takes place. All of the above comprise the assessment and all of the above are subjective, no matter how well they are disguised and said to be objective. Data gathered through interview or observations are easy to be seen as subjective. The fact that a professional is involved in the process doesn't make these findings any more objective. Individual psychologists see and interpret the world through the prism of a psychological perspective that is acquired from training and experience. Some subscribe to a traditional psycho-analytical perspective, others behavioral and cognitive. There are many others ranging from bioenergetics, where body type is seen as important, to Objects Relations, where the main perspective focuses on the idea that, "The apple doesn't fall far from the tree." So, clearly, what is being observed or heard depends upon how one filters that input.

The fact that most, if not all, of the tenets underlying psychological theory remains unproven, and in some cases, outright ridiculous, should give pause to anyone looking for recommendations based upon data obtained through psychological interview and observation. When it comes to psychological testing, here is where the real problem lies. Few, instruments, if any, that are used in psychological assessment are in any way capable of deciding which parent, if any, would be the better parent and in the best interest of the child. My experience is that pathological parental behaviors are far more obvious than psychological tests. Yet, judges have awarded custody to fathers who have engaged in frequent domestic violence and where psychological testing has not "demonstrated" pathological behaviors.

A particular problem with junk science making its way into custody evaluations and decisions is the much bandied about issue of Parental Alienation Syndrome, which its subscribers like to pass off as something that really exists as either a medical or psychological condition. It is not. Granted parents in divorce can act in ways that are not beneficial to the relationship between the other parent and the child. In many cases this acting out behavior may be seen as normal given the frequency that it occurs. However, PAS is not an illness—it may be a cute concept that some like to use to discredit a parent and influence a judge's decision—but this has not stopped evaluators from using PAS as a basis for their custody recommendation. An excellent review of PAS by Jennifer

Hoult [4] is an important resource that debunks PAS and puts it into its appropriate perspective.

Standards For Distributing Custody

As a policy, the growth of custody litigation and the use of mental health professionals doing custody evaluations have muddied the intent and manifest function of the family courts. The issue becomes how do we get back to ensuring the child's best interest. I am convinced that we should do away with custody evaluations by mental health professionals. I think a much better approach would be to develop a set of legal standards whereby a parent's behaviors can be assessed as they might relate to a custody decision.

Mental health professionals can still play a role in family court, but by focusing on what we do best. If there is an issue about the mental stability of a parent and enough evidence exists to require a mental health evaluation, then that is a proper role for our profession. This role will minimize unethical behaviors and focus on our strengths and on services we can rightfully and appropriately provide. Table 1 describes a set of behaviors that might be considered. The behaviors listed are merely examples as I am sure that others can find behaviors that are just as important and applicable.

Table 1

Examples of Behaviors Related to Determining Custody, with the behavior followed.

Behavior—Rationale
Substance Abuse—*Substance abusers are not able to act in the best interests of another person.*

Sexual, Physical, and Emotional Abuse—*Perpetrators of these behaviors are dangerous and cannot act as reasonable parents.*

Severe Mental Illness—*Severe mental illness affects all aspects of function, putting children at risk.*

History of Absent Parenting—*No reason to expect that things will change if parent gains custody.*

History of Bad Decision Ability—*Parenting requires consistent and appropriate decision making.*

History of Consistent Felonious Illegal Conduct—*Good parenting requires a good role modeling and maintaining a sound environment for children.*

Court Employed Panels

I would recommend that we do away with privately hired panels of custody evaluators. The present system provides too many opportunities for conflicts of interests and a lack of standards. For example, a team of mental health professionals would become court employees. Reasonable fees would be assessed for those who can pay and waived for those who cannot. Professionals who are employed by the court can receive appropriate training and randomly assigned to cases. Assessment standards must be an important part of any evaluation. I submit that this can be accomplished more effectively by standardized training and supervision. Professionals employed by the court can also be used in mediation services and other important aspects of family court matters.

Some may argue that panels employed by the court would not work because evaluators would become low waged professionals and subject to continual budget cutting. This would result in low morale and poor performance thus offsetting any positive benefits from the elimination of private evaluators. I do not think that this argument has any real merit because the same can be said of all other court employees. For example, if this argument held any validity then why not call for the privatization of judges? There is a compelling state and societal interest in maintaining a non-private judiciary. Likewise, as custody evaluators and consultants exist solely to provide the court with specific recommendations, they too, essentially, are part of the judiciary. Therefore, in my opinion, there is the same state and societal interest in having these professionals be free of conflicting interests. When left in private hands, the probability of conflicts of interests and dual relationships by custody evaluators is too high to be ignored.

Judicial Procedures and Custody Recommendations

Data gathering in a judicial proceeding is accomplished by well-established evidence gathering procedures. These are tasks that should be made by judges and the attorneys involved in the custody hearing. Depositions, subpoenas for documents, and other legal procedures typically are the way in which the court can evaluate the various arguments and requests made by attorneys for their clients. All the information that a custody evaluator provides to the court can be obtained through these various legal procedures. So why leave these important findings to a private evaluator?

I can find no reason to defend using private mental health professionals to make these recommendations. Yes, it may be less time consuming and less costly to let a psychologist or psychiatrist make these recommendations as opposed to judges and attorneys, but at what cost? Given that mental health professionals use totally non-judicial ways to reach conclusions means that people are being denied their basic legal rights that are protected when the judiciary must make a decision. There is no appeal from an incompetent evaluation. The best that can be expected is a complaint to a professional board, which in most cases, goes nowhere. Parents and children who have been harmed have little hope of gaining an appeal in custody cases. Thus, one solution is to have judges and attorneys do the work that they are being paid to do and to use mental health professionals to do what we do best. What we do not do best is make recommendations as to which parent deserves custody. This is a legal issue.

Concluding Remarks

I think that everyone agrees that the family court system is both broken and in dire need of reform. Clearly, most custody recommendations adhere to some system of reasonableness, but what we must understand is that sociological and psychological concepts that are typically utilized in courts are the product of a political process. Courts abide by laws and laws most frequently are a product of legislation. Legislation is a product of a political process that is affected by lobbying and clout. While we would like to think and behave like our professions are separate and above politics, family law, and every other body of law, largely is a result of a drawn out political process and subject to ideological demands as much as any other factors.. Therefore, any recommendations to fix this broken system necessarily will be through legislative action and subject to lobbying from every interested and affected party.

While there are many reasons why family court proceedings fall short, the fact that custody determination has become so adversarial and overly legalistic cannot be ignored. We expect the rights of parents to have legal counsel. Merely representing one side or the other does not constitute unethical behavior for attorneys. Nevertheless, being on the winning side may not be in the best interest of a child or the parents. For mental health professionals, however, there must be different rules of conduct. As

Socrates said two thousand years ago, "Being a good citizen does not necessarily mean being a good person." The point being that we can all behave according to the law and people made rules, but that does not automatically make us good people or mean we are doing the right thing.

While I will leave it to those practicing law to decide on how their behaviors need to change, I advocate that professional psychologists need to take radical and corrective action if we are to become part of the solution to a broken and ineffective system. Mental health professionals have no business rendering custody recommendations. We are clinical professionals. There are no states that I know of that provide separate licensing for forensic evaluators. Our primary training is in a clinical discipline and that is reflected in our licensing. Clearly, most, if not all forensic practitioners, have training in forensic practice. This is not the issue. By definition, a mental health professional can speak to and address mental, behavioral, and emotional issues. What a court decides to do with that information belongs in their domain. This is why we need to get away from trying to fit psychological theories into legal practice. They are distinct models of custody and are sociological, legal, and political. The psychological data is much too varied, complex, many times biased, but mostly unavailable and inappropriate to make the types of recommendations that are required. I just do not see how observing a person in a relatively short interview and administering a series of questionable tests allows one to render a recommendation that has such wide ranging affects. Above all, we must remember that determining issues of custody ultimately is a legal process. It is not our domain.

References

1. Melton, G., Petrila, J., Poythress, N., & Slobogin, C. (2007). *Psychological evaluations for the courts: A handbook for mental health professionals and lawyers* (3rd ed.) New York, NY: Guilford Press.
2. American Psychological Association (2010). Guidelines for Child Custody Evaluations in Family Law Proceedings. http://www.apa.org/practice/guidelines/child-custody.pdf.
3. Brave, SL, Ellman, IA, & Fabricius, WV. (2003). Relocation of Children After Divorce and Children's Best Interests: New Evidence and Legal Considerations. *J. of Family Psychology,* Vol. 17, No. 2, 206-219.
4. Hoult, J. (2006). The Evidentiary Admissibility of Parental Alienation Syndrome: Science, Law, and Policy. *Children's Legal Rights Journal,* Vol. 26, No. 1, 1-61.

Chapter 5

A Lawyer's View of Family Court Evaluations

Toby Kleinman, J.D.

DR. JANET CUMMINGS: Our next speaker is Ms. Toby Kleinman, who, among other things, has been voted a New Jersey Super Lawyer. She is a New Jersey lawyer, but has consulted on legal cases in at least 40 out of the 50 states. She has edited, she has published in law journals, and she is the Director of the Advisory Board to the Leadership Council on Child Abuse and Interpersonal Violence. She served as a professional liaison to the American Psychological Association and is invited constantly to give keynote addresses, lectures at colleges, and has appeared as an expert guest on network television. So we are most fortunate to have Ms. Kleinman with us.

MS. KLEINMAN: First of all, thank you. I am really honored to be here and to have been invited. I think this has been so far—and I know we have a whole day ahead of us—very interesting for me. I know time is limited, so I am going to just jump right in.

I was asked to talk about a lawyer's view of family court evaluations, so I am going to have, I think, a different perspective than you may hear from the psychologists.

When a trial lawyer is retained to represent anyone in a civil case or in a criminal case, a skilled and experienced lawyer usually can get a handle on the issues that will ultimately determine the outcome of the case. They can make a fair assessment of the probabilities of success on the very broad panorama of issues that are present and those that will be spawned during the course of litigation. And, ultimately, a lawyer can or usually reasonably can predict and give advice and project potential outcomes. And they can also tell the client what to expect down the road.

The one huge exception to this is in family court cases where there are issues of domestic violence and child abuse—or child abuse. To understand that skepticism, and I should say I will talk personally to it and to understand my skepticism in the private sector and of those of us who do child protection work, you have to take a step back to really understand the setting in which these evaluators are appointed and the powers that they are called upon to serve.

The family court procedures are based upon laws where the procedures as employed, and usually as ratified by the appellate courts, can easily and seriously undermine the intent of the statutes, which have been designed for victim protection. And as they do so, they are undermining the letter of the law as well as the intent of the law. This is true for many reasons, but one of the most critical reasons—and because I have a short time, I cannot go into most of the reasons—but one of the critical reasons is that in family courts we permit what we refer to as "relaxation of the rules of evidence" and other court rules. The purpose of that rule was to permit—I think it was Marjory Fields who said it was a social-work background—to permit a more thorough understanding by family court judges of the dynamic of a family and the issues that were raised. It was never intended to be relaxed so the court could delegate its responsibility to a court-appointed evaluator, especially to untrained court-appointed evaluators. So in many ways, these courts act as they are acting are essentially lawless: the relaxation of the rules that they do not have to follow, undermining completely the intent and the letter of the law.

The culture that existed when today's judges or their parents were growing up—so it was when they were raised—did not take domestic violence seriously. It was not until the mid-1950s, which sounds like a long time ago, but it truly wasn't, that actually all states removed women as chattel, or property, of their husbands to do with how they pleased. In the 1970s, the theory of the law was based upon the "tender years doctrine," but really what it was is that men did not want custody of their children, so it wasn't an issue of the courts that they had to deal with. So "tender years" was really convenient. It was used by the courts: women got custody. Men were not attacked. It was what they wanted. It was assumed, by virtue of the fact that children were of tender years, that they would be with their mother.

How It Changed in the 1980s: Unqualified Evaluators

Into the 1980s, it became acceptable in society for men to become custodial parents. And it began to change theories, and theories developed to try to support this, a la Richard Gardner and parent alienation syndrome, which was and is still nothing more than a theory that is inaccurate. But it got traction in the courts, and it became a basis for courts to rule. So they did so with unqualified, unscrupulous court-appointed evaluators who relied upon this junk science to assert that a father should have custody of his children, and issues of domestic violence got set aside.

Now, mind you, in the late '70s and early '80s at this time, domestic violence came to the forefront as an issue in the courts, and states had been enacting laws to protect women from spouse abuse. So this developed all at the same time. However, judges were never really trained on how to understand the dynamics of the abuse. They were trained in the law and on the law, and they continued to use discretion, make credibility determinations, and they often did so incorrectly, because real victims' behaviors are often counterintuitive and perpetrators of domestic violence do not resemble the monster that the judges would have expected. So training was lacking and the family court judges repeatedly gave fathers custody where issues of domestic violence were raised. And I am saying this "was." It still is true. The courts would appoint an evaluator. The judge would sometimes call these evaluators ex parte or the judge would have given many hints on the record of how skeptical they were of a woman's motives. The court-appointed evaluator would certainly get the message, and the reports would be clear and decisive: Give dad the kids. Teach mom a lesson. He is a friendlier parent.

At the same time this was going on, children were seen as but pawns of the parents, with no legal rights of protection, and this has not changed much, and I am going to talk a little bit about that tomorrow, so I am not going into it today. But after a period of time, in these cases, if the issue of child abuse arose, the court greeted those issues with even more skepticism, and more of the women, themselves, began to look—they begin to look askance at the women even worse than when domestic violence had been originally raised, because there was never proper training on how to discern whether or not child abuse had occurred, and it relied upon untrained, unqualified evaluators to "assist the court." Thus, competent lawyers in the private sector who work in the field of child custody are very often distrustful of evaluators appointed by family court. The lawyers attached to child protective service agencies, in a sense, are what I sometimes refer to as "silent partners" between the court. Because the agency lawyer, knowing what will be done at each intersection of the case, each expecting of the other to do its part to lead the court to enter the orders that each can predict in advance, even as the evaluators are used to move the case forward. Thus, all too frequently the issues of violence in the family—spouses and children alike—were not actually addressed in evaluators' reports in what we would want, which is a progressive manner, instead they used—understanding the legislation as written, based upon the scientific and informative knowledge of these issues of the day when they came before the court, because court-appointed evaluators were too often and are too often unqualified and they simplify the custodial issues.

I cannot help but interject here since I have represented many, many victims, and in many, many cases of child abuse, there is very frequently no corroborating evidence. And this is the ultimate of exasperation of actual victims, and it isn't sometimes until well after evaluators don't believe, after very scientific interviews and scientific evaluations, that something happens and something serious happens. So I do not find that quite enough. But it is part of an old culture, which continues today.

A case which should be the most demanding of the most credentialed, carefully trained, skilled forensic evaluators are often left to people who have little or no training in newly developed areas. And domestic violence and child abuse are the most critical of those areas.

So Dr. John Caccavale talked about the business, and I am going to talk a little bit about that in a moment. But one of the problems that we see often with these evaluators is also the fact that many of them have had no previous training or experience or clinical experience with the population they are being asked to examine. Or they may have done some clinical work, but rely on the courts to supplement their income and therefore experience.

Or they may have been doing years of custody evaluations, but never been trained on how to assess for domestic violence, never trained to assess on how to do child abuse. And absent the training, all the years of doing the custody evaluations is sometimes even more dangerous than having no experience with an honest and open-minded, but educated evaluator. These evaluators are acutely aware that courts are using them to help simplify resolution of the most difficult of issues of a possible divorce and to do so without a trial. Oh, hear that they settle more. They settle more. They settle more. Well, people who may have had years of experience doing custody evaluations may never have had the requisite training and experience, but the cases settle. They settle because that is what the courts are set up to have them do.

The Reports and Orders of the Court

The recommendations, more often than not, absent any testimony whatsoever, absent any cross-examination whatsoever, become the order for the court, even if it is in the interim of a case. And they often have misguided reasoning behind them. Some of those problems, such as domestic violence, are given short shrift because the evaluator has not been trained to assess. So, for example, whether or not—somebody asked this question earlier, I believe of Judge Marjory Fields—regardless—I think it was Dr. Ricky Greenwald who asked—whether or not domestic violence has ever been raised before. Even if it has been raised and denied as an order of a court, it needs to be assessed for if it is being raised. So you must have the requisite training. If a restraining order has been granted, then there is a finding. You have to—I agree with Judge Fields completely. You must have that as a fact. But where you do not have the requisite training, what these evaluators ought to be doing if they don't have it, is sending a woman for a battered woman's evaluation or a child abuse evaluation, someone with that very specialized training to give that information to them as a potential custody evaluator. But what they do, because part of this is a pecuniary interest—or a lot of it is—they keep it to themselves. And the finding and the recommendation they make are without proper scientific foundation and are often then doomed for failure, even though the courts will enter it, enter their recommendations.

The reports often explain away behavior or do not deal with it at all. They unscientifically blame the mother for a child's fear of the father or excuse the stated fear of father because a child seems comfortable in the father's presence, often accepting blindly the same language used by the batterer as to why the woman is paranoid, delusional, and on and on. Most importantly, for some unknown reason, the actual knowledge base of the science itself is at that point to become completely disregarded, and when one looks at the resume of the evaluator, it would have made clear that that person had no specialized knowledge or training.

In my review of reports, in my reading of reports, I look for internal consistency, and these evaluators are often left at odds within their own reports. Because there is no trial or cross-examination, that does not come out often until many months, sometimes years later, when a divorce is finalized. I hate the term "high conflict" because at least in my personal anecdotal experience it is never a high conflict because that talks about equal power, and we are not—when there is domestic violence, it isn't people of equal power we are talking about. We are talking about a power tilt. If we are talking about a protective parent and a child who is being abused, we are talking about a power tilt. So it isn't a high-conflict circumstance. It is a domestic violence circumstance. There is only about 1-2%—of all cases that are litigated, and we know that upwards of 90% of those have issues of domestic violence and/ or child abuse within them. Statistically, we also know across this country that 65% of the women who have raised child abuse during a custody litigation lose their children. Something is wrong.

So even when we have testimony, which often happens very late on in the game, the judges end up relying upon evaluators who admit their lack of credentials. They shouldn't testify on the custody at all if they had not training for sex abuse in domestic violence if those issues were raised, and they have done the evaluation in a subpar way and not acceptable to practice. I cannot tell you how many reports I have read where sex abuse was raised and yet the young child was brought to an interview by the named perpetrator. What? I mean, I know that as a lawyer. Take a deep breath. I'm sorry.

Assumptions that Ignore the Science: The So-Called Right to Parent

They make assumptions about the fear, the child's fear, contrary to what is known in science about children's reactions. They ignore disclosures of children and put them onto the protective parent, accusing the parent of coaching. They ignore the science that rapport-building is critical and it is the initial first step before a child would disclose to you, and instead of spending the time to build that rapport and taking the time to do so, they assume a lie or a cheat or a fraud, and they become part of the attack machine, accepting the other parent's formulation. I query: In what other realm of the law is a denial of a crime accepted as truth? And where else do we ever move on as though it is true? There is not a single area in the law except with child sex abuse, except with domestic violence.

There are other issues as well. The notions of reunification of the family or reorganizing the family to allow quality time with any parent who expresses an interest overrides plain risks of danger and facts which show history of danger, all of which are always present where there has been domestic violence. The idea of quality time with an abuser is romanticized, and the bar is set ridiculously low for contact and an opportunity to continue to abuse children and coerce them in the entirety of the circumstance.

And this is so because the Constitution of the United States has been interpreted to mean the parents have a right to parent. It's so, because looking at a man accused of battering when he is standing before you in a three-piece suit is counterintuitive to believe that he could do that, and there isn't proof; there are no pictures, not necessarily any broken bones. It is ignored because, looking at that man accused by his child of heinous acts of sexual abuse, it is easier to believe that he didn't do it and the wife is making the child say it. And I am reminded of a father I cross-examined in a courtroom years ago about heinous acts against the child of his first wife. He was then married, and the issue was involving another child. And as I cross-examined him—I had an affidavit of that child—and I questioned him on each act. And I must say I had a bit of a hard time containing myself as I asked each question. And he admitted all those heinous acts—pornography, nightly basis; rape, nightly basis—from the time the child was 4 years old. He testified, actually testified, that the Statute of Limitations had run on these crimes, and of course he knew that; he was a lawyer. The crimes were committed in another state. I almost vomited. Sorry. I mean, I don't mean to be vulgar here. But it was really hard as he continued to admit, and I persisted and asked, and he cried. He cried. And he said, as he looked at the judge through his crocodile tears, "No, Your Honor, when I wasn't doing those things, I was a really good father. Ninety-nine percent of the time, I was a good father. And I didn't do anything to this child." And the judge looked at him—I mean, I still cannot get over this—this was a presiding family court judge in not my own state, another state—and he said, "I believe you, Mr. [So-and-So]." Mr. So-and-So was a lawyer, working for the federal government. Truly, had he not dropped dead running, the court may very well have given him visitation. But as it was, we had had it stopped and he died.

So where a court seeks to interfere with the parental rights, the child's safety must be in jeopardy, and therein lies the rub. Well, a child's safety is supposed to trump the parents' rights. The question very often for the court becomes a quantitative analysis of risk of harm. And most judges just do not get it. And it is within that framework that they are appointing evaluators.

The Safety of the Child

Critical to all of this is the fact that the children have no standing to object to who evaluates them, no standing to object to any recommendation or any orders that are entered. Laws that are designed to protect them are ignored. They can be ignored because it's relaxed, and they are ignored. And courts in their appointments can override or ignore expert opinions where there are safety concerns expressed and/or issues of lethality of abusers, even when they exist, even where an evaluator has opined that there is a risk of danger to the child.

Courts universally place the safety of the child as a subset to the litigation between the parents in a divorce case. Safety is legislated as paramount, but the only way to do that is ignored; that is, child abuse and safety should be heard before any other issue gets determined. Rules of evidence must be followed and adhered to as to qualifications for testimony on issues of expertise of the person testifying, and the court should not be subjective in its approach to that science.

Agencies with investigative mandates of child abuse also have a mandate to protect children. Simultaneous to that, they seek to ensure the sanctity of the family unit. Thus, they are the prosecution and the defense, and the abusive parent is essentially given protection in an unarticulated and broad parental interest in the recommendations to the court. So even where protective service agencies are brought in, their dual mandate conflicts with their overriding caution of child safety. If these same children were victims of stranger violence, I dare say these same people would express outrage, not seek to rejoin a relationship between the adult and the child. The lawyers who handle those matters then are also silent partners of the court system.

So where family courts are permitted to relax the rules, reportedly to protect the safety, in actuality, these rules are often used to appoint and then permit unqualified, unskilled people to testify, thereby perpetuating the harm to children. The child protective service lawyers know this, and sometimes rely on it to protect children, and at other times, they use it to dismantle their protection. It can only stop if it completely stops being permitted.

Family Courts: A Different Set of Rules

Family courts perpetuate a different set of court rules and rules of evidence. The breadth of the problem in court, as I have explained, frequently centers on the lack of qualification, in part because if they hear no broken bones or see no broken bones, the courts do not necessarily understand it. One has to wonder when we see the recent Joe Paterno major scandal in which he did not report what he knew. Did he do nothing because he did not think it was bad? Did the man who told Paterno ignore it himself and not go to the police because he was afraid? Afraid of what? Of power? Imagine—imagine the power to a child. Parent's power over a child. Imagine that power dynamic with a battered spouse or any spouse worried for a child's safety, and then they are faced with the court appointing someone unqualified, never sending it to a prosecutor, and blaming the mother for coaching. Why would anyone come forward?

These mothers are brave. These mothers need to bring this all out in the open, and the system and the policies need to change, because children's rights do not exist in any substantive way that we would equate with stranger violence when a child discloses abuse or when a woman is a victim of violence by a spouse.

An abusive parent does not face the same rigors of evidence as exist with stranger violence. In criminal court, because there is no concession does not mean there will not be a prosecution now, does it? But in family courts, every day we drop the issue because the perpetrator says, "I didn't do it, Your Honor. She's lying." We know that clinical interviews are not really scientific, and so if you are dealing with an unqualified expert and they are not coming under any scrutiny, what then do you have. There is no crime where someone interviews the defendant, and relies upon a denial as sufficient to fail to prosecute. But unqualified experts rely, and then the courts rely on them. Very often the women are coming apart at the seams. They are at loose ends, often angry, appropriately, at the spouse and at the court. Many of these evaluators are unqualified to even diagnose post-traumatic stress disorder. And I have come to find that their diagnoses are borderline and paranoid because nobody really looks at it. These people are unqualified. So where a woman's reactions are actually adaptive behaviors or part of post-traumatic stress and as a result of years of battering, the evaluator finds the abuser easier to deal with and relates to a man smiling up at them than a woman who is at loose ends. The unqualified evaluator shifts their focus to how to promote a better understanding between the parents, when we would never have two strangers ever speak to each other after violence occurred between them, nor would we ever allow our child to be with a neighbor again if a neighbor had abused the child.

So safety for the child has often shifted too: Go along, get along, ignore a child's pleads, the mother is told, or you will lose your child; you will lose custody. Indeed, the impact of the violence, much less the violence, has all been ignored.

And then courts become even more skeptical if there is an agreement and the issues get raised later, because there has already been the belief that the abuse did not happen, everything is based on that false belief, and the predisposed thinking takes hold, and the process itself starts not with the question of what happened here, but with confirmatory bias that it did not happen, and it sets forth why is she raising these issues rather than openly exploring what actually happened. And they stop contact with the mother, where they never would have even suspended visitation with the father when a child made a disclosure.

I would just say in closing, there are three things that we need that are critical. I mean, we need massive reform. I have said a lot of what—or I have talked about, but the final piece is that the standards are not the problem. It is really the implementation of the standards and the accountability that goes along with that.

And I thank you very much.

Chapter 6

Appropriate Language to Use in Family Court to Protect Children

Toby Kleinman, J.D.

DR. JANET CUMMINGS: Welcome back Toby Kleinman, New Jersey super lawyer and pit bull for the rights of women and children.

MS. KLEINMAN: Are you tired of me yet?

VOICES: No!

MS. KLEINMAN: Well, I am here to talk now about the importance of domestic violence sensitive language. And what a court says—I have a feeling you probably know everything I am about to say, but I am going to say it anyway. I don't know that this is—I should be saying this—Janet, you don't want me to do this, but I have feeling that it may end up being somewhat interactive, and if people want to interrupt me, I am easily interrupted. So please—you know, stand up, and I will recognize you if there is something that it evokes.

What a court says to a litigant during a custody or visitation litigation has a significant impact on the litigant and on the course of litigation. The most natural language for a judge to use stems from the Constitution. I talk a lot about the Constitution. However, language that may appear on its face to express equal rights and equal protection under the law may actually be communicating the opposite and setting the stage for the perpetrator of domestic violence to feel emboldened by the court.

Paradoxically, such language creates a sense of disempowerment to victims of domestic violence. Thus, to guarantee equal protection also requires a special sensitivity to the impact of language on these parties in court.

I have a son who is an actor who always says to me: You know, one of the actor's most difficult jobs is that there's really two parts to every communication. It is what you say and how it is received, and the actor has that job, so does a judge, to make sure that what they intend to say is communicated in the way it is intended and that it is also received by each person in that way. So the nuances of the words utilized have significant impact on both the victims and the perpetrators, and it is important for the court and others in the court to use language that will accurately reflect and communicate to both the victim and the perpetrator.

To properly understand its impact, it is helpful to have an overview of the setting in which the language will be used as well as the process that is taking place. So picture this scenario where the parties have separated as a result of domestic violence. While domestic violence is not gender-specific, it is gender-predominant against females and children, as we have been talking about, also the elderly, but I am not here now talking about the elderly. Thus, I am going to refer to the male as the perpetrator and the female as the victim.

Here is Your Scenario:

The wife has been granted a restraining order where, after an evidentiary hearing, a judge has made a finding that there has been domestic violence and the husband has been removed from the marital residence. The husband has been the primary financial support of the family. The wife has had the responsibility for the day-to-day care of the children. While she has also held a job, she earns far less than her husband and thus is dependent upon the husband for most of the family support. The wife still lives in the marital residence, using her salary as well as the support she gets from her husband and is responsible to pay the family's bills, hers and the children's. Because she earned far less than her husband during the marriage, the wife has virtually had all of the responsibility to handle also all of the children's extracurricular activity—doctors, dentists, orthodontia appointments—as well as making social arrangements for the children, transporting the children to and from school, and helping with the homework.

Once the parties are in court, there is an expectation that both parents should set aside their differences for the welfare of the children. Thus, we find phrases such as, "These two parents need to learn how to get along." When the perpetrator hears that phrase, it is a very clear message that the court does not understand—in fact, does not even have a clue—of the power he has over his wife, and he feels emboldened and he feels empowered. The words may actually encourage abuse of power over his wife during the litigation of custody or control over finances. For certain, he knows how to gain control because he knows his wife's fears. In addition, he knows whether he has used the threat of taking custody of their children, as domestic violence perpetrators often do, to maintain control of their wives during the marriage.

To the domestic violence victim, his wife, those same words from the judge's lips tell her that the court does not understand that the victim's husband cannot negotiate. She hears that this judge doesn't have a clue that this isn't a negotiation. This is power. His way is to demand compliance and capitulation through the use of intimidation, violence, name-calling, attacks on her directly, and through others as crazy and/or threats. She knows that the only way to gain equality is for the court to have an understanding of her husband and to use the court's power to secure her equality. Thus, the victim hearing those words is fearful and has more of a sense of helplessness than she had before. She now knows she may be at risk of more violence so she must be hyper-vigilant. The victim sees the court as having power over her husband that she did not have, and she, as a result of that language, begins to see them as allies and feels overpowered and alone, and she is.

Before coming to court, she anticipated that the court would use its authority to protect her and her children. Domestic violence language, sensitive language, sorry, can assure that both parents receive their equal protection under the law, but that the court can use its power to let the perpetrator and the victim know that the long-term—that they understand the long-term impact of violence in the home and can speak directly to this issue. For example, a judge can state: I hope you understand the importance of not trying to use the court to control your wife, as I will not tolerate it. The children need to be assured of that protection to the full extent of the law. The children may or may not have seen your violence to your wife, but they are victims of it nevertheless, and I know it. Surely your wife behaved differently than she would have had she not feared that you would continue to hurt her. If nothing else, the children are aware of that. They are entitled to have two parents who are free from violence, and I intend to make sure that occurs.

That same judge can look to the domestic violence victim and state—again, this is instead of "we expect you to get along"— "While I am aware of your husband's ability to control you or try to use the court to control you, it is important for me to try to have you understand, my role is to allow the children to have the best relationship possible with both of you. To that end, I am going to ask you to try to overcome some of your fears at least in the presence of the children to the extent that you can." Such oratory recognizes the perpetrator's power and ability to control, while still acknowledging the domestic violence victim's difficulty in encouraging any positive relationship.

I will say anecdotally, I have never found a victim in all the years that I have been doing this that was not willing to try. They usually try without even being asked because they see that that is their role. So when a judge says that, it does not usually really change anything. All it does is say: This is a safe place for me to come. That is really what is being communicated. But what it does is it also creates a new power structure because the victim then understands, I can come back to this person when things aren't working. And the husband, the perpetrator, knows, if the judge says what he needs to say, that the court will use its power to continue to protect the wife and will use its power to protect the children. And many states require parents to try to negotiate visitation even where there has been domestic violence findings. So it is even more important in that circumstance that a court communicate correctly and tell both parents something to the order of this: The children have already been hurt by what you have done in the home. I will use my power to keep that from happening again. I will keep coercive parenting from being perpetrated on these children even if you have visitation. This state takes seriously its obligation to protect children from emotional harm— witnessing or experiencing verbal abuse, name-calling, putdowns of the mother or the children—will cause harm and this court will not tolerate it at all.

And I am not personally here encouraging negotiation, and I suggest that judges say that to mothers: I am not encouraging you, but I want you to know that this court is a friendly place to victims. And I want you, Father, to know that your parental rights do not give you any rights to hurt emotionally or physically your children or your wife. The message again is very clear: If you are fearful or there are threats to you, come to me. I will take them seriously. Tell your lawyer; you're pro se, come back to me, tell me. I will take that very seriously.

It also gives the message to the perpetrator that the court is not afraid to stop contact if they do not behave. Another problem that occurs during litigation where there is sole custody is that many states encourage joint custody and joint decision-making. This is illogical to believe that someone who uses coercive control and threats as a matter of control will simply stop voluntarily. Nevertheless, courts all too frequently lose sight of this piece of human nature as it becomes impossible to negotiate with the husband, the perpetrator. I have heard countless judges comment almost offhandedly—and I said this before—if this woman wants to spend all of the marital funds to litigate—and I must say each time I hear that I cringe, I recognize that this little phrase translates into a lack of consideration for a victim's inability to negotiate with her abuser. It signifies a victim's failure to recognize the impact of domestic violence on children.

The Impact of Language

Judges also need to be particularly sensitive to the things they say, as they may actually be opening the door for the perpetrator to repeat a phrase that was once used maybe intentionally innocently by a court. That same type of phrase becomes a put-down to the victim for her to assure her children's safety.

There is no qualification, for example, that the children will only be protected from strangers in the Constitution. If a parent truly believes children need protection from the other parent or if one parent uses the children as a sword against the other, which is what we see in these cases, sole custody, even in traditionally joint custody jurisdictions, is actually necessary, essential for that family. When the victim seeks sole custody in this circumstance, they need a court to support that. This is true—especially when we see and the courts see that they are spending a lot of money. It should become apparent to a court that something is going awry, because the women are tapping these funds because they believe it is essential to protect their children, not because they want to spend the money, especially, again, where there is domestic violence.

There is another issue here that is seldom understood by judges: Domestic violence sensitive language requires an understanding of the need for a victim to have financial independence in order to remove the perpetrator's control. It requires the use of the court's contempt powers to assure a perpetrator's compliance with judicial orders that are issued because the court must be steadfast in its support for the victim. The abuser may disagree, but the court is required to enter orders requiring support and visitation, and sometimes that requires that the financial control be removed from the male and given to the female. So instead of saying—money can be taken right from jobs, and can be taken and given directly, and in some states now, we have that automatically so that the victims of domestic violence or any person in a child support matter gets the money directly, and there is a system in place where they do not actually have to go and ask for money, but it is withdrawn so as long as there is somebody working. There are circumstances that can become more difficult, but that is another way of doing it.

The impact of language is also felt on how society views the separate parental roles of mothers and fathers, and this is really important to understand, because fathers who seek custody are somehow seen as noble or romantic in trying to co-parent, because society still gives, or seems to give extra value to a father who wants to spend time parenting. On the other hand, a woman is expected to want to parent, so she receives no special recognition at all. It is her duty, after all. She's a mother.

Domestic violence sensitive language would give a woman proper credit with a historically female job of raising the children and the difficult tasks ahead. Such language would also pierce any romantic notion about a father seeking to parent and look to the father's actual participation as a parent prior to the marital breakdown. Domestic violence sensitive language requires the recognition that the perpetrator is suspect, suspect for wanting a sudden change in amount of time and responsibility from the level of participation he had prior to a divorce proceeding. Statements such as "We should be happy he wants to spend time with the kids" or "Aren't the kids lucky to have a father willing to spend more time with them" should not go without scrutiny. Sensitivity to both parents and their children requires essentially determining what the status quo was before the marital separation, before the relationship came to court, because security for the children includes ensuring that they experience the least amount of disruption in their lives. This would likely mean keeping them in the same school, same home, the same ability to maintain friendships and to have similar time with each parent they had, as long as it is in a safe environment, before the separation.

A romantic view of fathers' active parenting is not appropriate where there is domestic violence. Language used by the court or experts that does not recognize the inequality of power and control is not domestic violence sensitive. Frequently, we still hear issues of estrangement, accusations of alienation. Where there is an accusation in the context of a domestic violence history it is even more important for the court to use sensitive language. As the starting point, the judge should question the parent who is alleging this alienation or estrangement about the familial arrangement for childcare before the breakdown of the marriage. And I would dare say, anecdotally, it has virtually been the mother. These guys do not and have not participated in a very, very profound way before the breakdown. It's new. And once a judge knows that, it is critically important. So if the mother was in fact the children's primary caregiver throughout the marital relationship and there was then domestic violence before already saying there was finding, the judge can recognize, then, it is appropriate for the victim to feel angry, maybe even outraged, because the father, previously uninvolved father, suddenly wants total or shared custody when he couldn't care less what happened at the last 3:30, whatever, doctor's appointment.

Negative Inferences

Often courts draw a negative inference if an alleged victim has never called the police about violence. Similarly, the court should ask the perpetrator: Why now are you seeking to spend more time with your children? It is appropriate to suspect his motivation where there is a sudden shift. It must be considered as a part of the power and control paradigm. Where children are thriving with their mother's care status quo, mom as the custodian, a court needs to recognize that if the children are suddenly now with the perpetrator at times when they were not previously with him, it might be pleasant for him, but it is not the status quo. Frequently courts view as negative a victim's appropriate anger at being victimized instead of accepting anger as a natural consequence, and the court should not use any punishment, reprisal, or angry language with a victim who is angry as a result of being a victim. Instead, sensitivity to her status as a victim includes understanding her reasonable basis for her anger. Again, I liken this to stranger violence or a stranger to be victimized, everyone would, and not a single person would not recognize that anger would be appropriate. In fact, if she wasn't angry, you would think something was wrong with her.

Domestic Violence and Manipulative Anger

The same standard must be applied to victims of domestic violence. Use of sensitive language requires thinking outside the realm of family court and an analysis similar to stranger-perpetrator-victim model. For example, in criminal law, we take victim impact statement. Victims participate in plea negotiations because the victim's anger is accepted, understood as appropriate. And in this way, the need to protect the child from the abuser would be clear to anyone who hears the facts.

Likewise, in visitation orders, the court should use the same analogy involving violence to a stranger in considering a child's reaction to a person they know is capable of violence. You know, if I smash a table or hit someone else and a child sees or knows that happened, they see that person who happens to be their parent and say, "I'm next. I could be next. What do I need to do to not make that happen?" So already we have created stress, a child who is accommodating to a bad situation. If it happened with a stranger, the need to protect the child would be obvious.

I have frequently heard what I refer to as manipulative anger. It is spoken in a manner by a perpetrator designed to show he is incredulous, indignant, and I am then reminded of the case where a child was abused in the attic of the family home. You probably all know this case. When the alleged perpetrator was asked about this, he denied going to the attic. He was angry at the question and never went to the attic. Do you know who I am talking about?

If there was no abuse, why did he not answer instead that he would never abuse this child? The nuances of such responses are important if courts are to be domestic violence sensitive. Some people do not understand why charges are not brought when there has been violence—and I am not going to go through that again. But even where a judge is sensitive, there is the much overlooked factor of judges handling as many as 1,000 cases a year and sometimes more. There are some counties in New Jersey I think that 2,000 cases cross a judge's desk. There is little time for each. And, in addition, while court orders are designed for finality, a family's needs are in flux, creating a dynamic between the court and the family that is sometimes pretty inconsonant.

And I just want to say that I know there are judges sitting here at this conference. But this is something as lawyers, as family advocates, as therapists to be aware of, because you write reports or you are talking to people, and the other side, the how you receive, how what you say is received is so critical, and that is true whether it is in family therapy, in child therapy, in court orders in the use of language, and basically every facet of everything we have been talking about. Think about not only what you are saying, what you are trying to communicate, but how it will be received.

Thank you.

Chapter 7

Risk Assessment in Family Court Evaluations

David L. Shapiro, Ph.D.

DR. JANET CUMMINGS: Our next speaker is a forensic psychologist and professor at Nova Southeastern University. He teaches such things as forensic assessment, criminal law, and professional ethics. He is doing research on a new inventory, the Power and Control Inventory, which he will be talking about and, I believe, has copies out in the lobby for those who are interested. He is a prolific writer and practitioner. He consults on criminal and civil cases. He has been involved in assessing risk for violence, neuropsychological screenings, and a number of other issues. Most importantly, he has the privilege of being married to Dr. Lenore Walker. So welcome Dr. David Shapiro.

DR. SHAPIRO: Thank you, Janet. Thank you, all. I am going to have a somewhat different approach. I am going to spend some time with you on some research regarding risk assessment. Now you might say, why is risk assessment relevant to these issues? Well, we are talking about not only domestic violence, but who is it that perpetrates domestic violence? Is there a way of identifying those who will perpetrate domestic violence in the future? This is the whole area of what we call "risk assessment."

As I was thinking about this and thinking about the theme of this conference, broken family courts, it occurred to me that one of the things that goes on when we talk about risk assessment, with perpetrators of domestic violence, is that there is an underlying assumption that we really know who it is, the types of people that do perpetrate domestic violence. In fact, as I hope to demonstrate to you, very little is known about this population. The research in this area is pathetic. It is very, very limited. Dr. Janet Cummings did mention I am trying to do some research in the area. I have developed what I call the Power and Control Inventory. I have copies of it out on the table in front. Please feel free to help yourself to it. It is in the process of being validated. Anybody who works with batterers who would like to help me develop some validation data, please, pick it up, use it, send me your results. I would really like to have that.

But when we talk about this whole idea of violence risk assessment in family law matters, I am reminded of a law professor with whom I have worked over the past several years. Some of you may know a law professor by the name of Michael Perlan. He has developed a concept called "pretextualism." And pretextualism is pervasive throughout the mental health law area. We go under the pretext that we have well-trained evaluators, using well-validated instruments to give informed decisions to the courts regarding the best interests of the child.

In fact, none of those assumptions are true. And, yet, we keep going—and this is one of the many reasons—that I think that the system is broken, because we go on these pretexts and just reinforce these pretexts over and over again, that we have valid instruments, that we are making valid determinations that are of value to the court.

I want to discuss some very early research. As I said before, we are really at a point in which we are trying to start some research. The research up to this point is really very poor. The whole idea about assessment of violence is, believe it or not, of fairly recent origin. Some of you may know this. Prior to, say, about 1985, assessment of violence was done purely on a clinical basis. Someone would sit down, talk to somebody, and come up with a conclusion as to whether or not this person was potentially violent. At that point, it was also actually called "prediction of dangerousness," whatever "dangerousness" was. A researcher by the name of John Monahan in the early 1980s started publishing some very disturbing research—or actually what we call now meta analyses—showing that clinicians were in fact wrong two out of three times in their assessments of the potential for violent behavior, that we were absolutely very poor in our ability to predict violent behavior. Monahan became the principal investigator for a large-scale research project under the auspices of The MacArthur Foundation, which lasted for about 20 years, and accomplished a large number of things, much too detailed for me to go into. But one of the things they came up with was to expand the range of predictor and criterion variables, predictive variables. Before, it was just a clinical interview. Ultimately, The MacArthur Foundation research identified five different areas in which these parameters that needed to be taken into effect: demographic, sociological, psychological, biological, and contextual variables. And they studied each one of these areas. They ultimately came up with 38 different domains that they said were relevant to violence risk assessment.

There was also, then, a conceptual shift away from prediction of dangerousness to how much risk is involved when you look across all these parameters. One of the very controversial areas was the role of mental illness in this. What ultimately came out of this and other research were several different approaches to the assessment of violent behavior. One we have already talked about, the purely clinical approach.

Secondly, there began developing in the late 1980s into the mid-1990s what we call the actuarial assessment of violent behavior. This is where certain static, fixed factors, such as whether or not somebody grew up in an intact household, whether or not there was substance abuse in the family, whether there was evidence of maladjustment in the early school years. These were taken as static variables, entered into an actuarial equation, and out of this allegedly came a predictive variable of how likely this person was to be violent. Some people who were uncomfortable with that went to what they call an adjusted actuarial, where they would modify some of these variables in terms of clinical insights.

And, finally, the most recent approach is what is called "structured professional judgment." Structured professional—or structured clinical judgment is where you take, say, an area of research, like the MacArthur research—say it identified 38 areas that need to be looked at—you use those as kind of a guide as a way of structuring your evaluation, making sure you are covering all of these different areas. But then within each of the areas, you can use your clinical judgment to pursue different leads. So it is sort of a guideline.

Now, one of them, for instance, is called the HCR, which stands for Historical, Clinical, and Risk factors and, interestingly, all of these schemes—and I am going to come back to this later— have the concept of psychopathy involved. The psychopath, the person who is cunning, manipulative, cannot learn from experience, has no empathy, this was a group of individuals that in every one of these predictive schemes seemed to be very heavily weighted in terms of the prediction of violent behavior.

Now, the question is: How much of this is relevant, if at all, to assessment of domestic violence? Well, the sad thing is:

not great. Okay? None of these schemes really hold up very well when you are trying to assess the potential for domestic violence.

Domestic Violence Risk Assessment Guide (DVRAG)

About five or six years ago, there was the first attempt to do an actuarial assessment of the potential for domestic violence. And this was the—what was called DVRAG, the Domestic Violence Risk Assessment Guide. I am not going to cover all of the things, so let me just highlight a few things. And, first of all, one of the things I would like you folks, please, I would like you to keep in mind for future discussion, as I go through these variables—and these are regarded as not based on clinical judgment, but actually correlated with recidivism, with domestic violence recidivism—please think of your own practices. Please think of the people with whom you have been in contact, both in terms of perpetrators and victims, and ask yourself: Do these factors really seem to be relevant?

Again, I am not going to go in detail over them, but this system has four items that deal with prior history of assault, whether or not the person has been sentenced to incarceration, and whether or not they have failed when they have been on conditional release. They have got one item involving threats to harm or kill the victim; one item about confining them, actually imprisoning them within a home or other facility; two areas having to do with children: the number of children between the perpetrator and the victim had together and then the number of the victim's children from prior relationships.

Then the consideration whether there is violence in other relationships outside of the victim and the perpetrator. Interestingly, that is the dimension, the parameter, that is most highly weighted in this Domestic Violence Risk Assessment Guide.

Whether or not there is substance abuse, whether or not there was an assault while the woman was pregnant, and the number of barriers to victim's support. In other words, did they live in an isolated area where their phone or internet connection such that the woman could be in contact with other people, and, again, finally, the score on the psychopathy checklist.

So in all of those different variables, you can see each one has a classification. If it is not applicable, it gets a one, or a score of zero, and each of them has a weight assigned to it. Add up all the weights, you put the weights into a formula, and you come out with a predictive value of the potential for domestic violence. So, again, maybe we can discuss this later on, but I would like you to think of these things again in terms of whether these really make sense in terms of your practice.

Spousal Assault Risk Assessment (SARA)

All right, folks, while you do this, I am going on to the next category, which is a risk assessment instrument called the "SARA," which stands for Spousal Assault Risk Assessment.

Now, the SARA is not an example of an actuarial instrument. Rather, it is one of these structured professional judgment instruments. In other words, the variables here are those that have been shown by the research to be relevant to the potential for domestic violence. How you inquire about that is up to your clinical judgment and your clinical skills.

So it has two items dealing with past assault, one assault of family, and one assault of strangers. And again, there is the item that shows up in the other ones, the past violation of conditional release. Two items having to do with relationship and employment problems, one having to do with being a victim of or a witness to family violence when growing up, an item dealing with substance abuse, another item dealing with suicidal or homicidal ideation, one dealing with psychotic symptoms, another dealing with personality disorder symptoms characterized by anger, impulsivity, and behavioral instability. Four items having to do with physical assault, sexual assault, and whether weapons were used and whether there were credible threats of death involved and whether there were violations of "no contact" orders.

Another dimension has to do with whether or not there was a recent escalation with either the severity or the frequency. And then finally two items having to do with an individual who minimizes or denies their assault history, and then attitudes that support or condone assault. And, of course, this gets into a lot of the stuff that I will talk about in a moment having to do with some of the research on the Power and Control Inventory. So that is the SARA.

These are attempts at domestic violence instruments. I am sorry to say they are not really great. There is some more with the SARA, and we will come back to this later. I have sort of rearranged some of these issues.

Danger Assessment Scale

Another recent approach has been from a researcher by the name Jacquelyn Campbell. Some of you may know Dr. Campbell's work. She takes a rather interesting approach, and in Jacquelyn Campbell's research, she says that the woman's perception of how serious the threat is or how credible the threat is, that is the single most important variable in determining the severity of possible abuse. In other words, the woman's subjective perception of danger, which, as you can see, does not appear in any of these other risk assessment schemes, while Jacquelyn Campbell's work puts a lot of focus on the woman's subjective perception. She says it is the best single predictor of re-assault, and when abuse has been documented, it is the best single predictor of lethality; that is, that the perpetrator will act out and actually kill the woman.

Dr. Campbell's assessment instrument is broken into three parts. In the first part, there is a rating of the different kinds of assaults, all the way from slapping and pushing, all the way up to the use of a weapon so seriously that it causes actual injury. In part two, the woman who fills this out is asked to respond "yes" or "no" to whether there is physical assault or physical violence that increases in severity and frequency, whether there is choking, possession of guns, forced sex, use of street drugs, or daily threats to kill.

Part three, asks yes or no to, whether the perpetrator tries to control their daily activities. Are there beatings while she has been pregnant, pervasive problems of jealousy, either threatened or attempted suicide on the part of the perpetrator such as, "You know, if you do not go along with this, I'll kill myself." And importantly, whether there has been violence to the children.

Now, this is the most interesting part of Dr. Campbell's research, some of the statistics. What she does is to add up all of these different categories. The average woman who—if there is such a thing—say the prototypical victim of abuse scored somewhere about a 3 on those, will endorse above 3, maybe slightly more of those items. If there is a score of 4 or greater, it is regarded a great risk, and a score of 8 or greater, lethal risk.

There are also some interesting statistics that come from the Department of Justice. If the woman is threatened or assaulted with a gun, the possibility of a violent death is 20 times more likely, if they are thus threatened and there is an actual assault. If she is threatened with a gun, but there is no actual assault, 15 times as likely. If the perpetrator chokes her, 10 times as likely. If there is pervasive jealousy, 9 times. Forced sexuality, 8 times. Possession of a gun, 6 times as likely.

I just want to make reference that, according to Dr. Campbell's research, 30% of the cases involving domestic violence lead to actual death or murder-suicides, 30%. And, as Dr. Walker mentioned, she and another one of our colleagues at Nova are trying to do some research in this area. I can't recall if she mentioned that South Florida has the dubious distinction of being the highest in the nation in terms of murder-suicide.

DOVE

I am running short on time so there were a number of other violence risk assessment schemes: one called the DOVE, which breaks the issue down into 19 variables. I will not go into these in any detail, primarily because of the lack of time, but also because a lot of them seem to cover the same dimensions.

Dr. Janet Johnson's assessment has nine predictor variables. One of the interesting areas, the police department in the city of Nashville, Tennessee, circulates a domestic violence risk assessment sheet, if you will, for people who are victims of domestic violence to help identify, and to help structure interventions. They identify a dimension that has not been covered in the rest of these, a sense of narcissism and entitlement on the part of the perpetrator. It is interesting that a police department plus, as we will assume that they had psychological consultants that helped them, came up with that dimension. But that does interface with a lot of the stuff that you will see, again hopefully if you pick up this Power and Control Inventory.

Domestic Violence Homicide Risk Assessment

I will give just a few words about the United States Department of Justice Domestic Violence Risk Assessment. This is some research that I am currently involved in, and I would love to have you help me with it. It basically covers the following dimensions: emotional control, discipline, financial control, isolation, sense of authority, sense of insecurity, substance abuse, and sexual jealousy. In knowing the population we are dealing with, I also have incorporated into this what I call a fake good scale, because none of these guys are going to say, "Yes, I do all of these things." So, you know, I have incorporated what I call a fake good scale.

In conclusion, let me just make a few remarks. First of all, domestic violence risk assessment has to be an ongoing dynamic process. The idea of doing it just at one point and resting on those results is just not going to work. So that really throws the whole idea of an actuarial assessment somewhat up in the air, because actuarial assessments are static variables by definition, variables that do not change.

When you get into the treatment, obviously one size does not fit all. There are different kinds of domestic violence. There are different kinds of batterers. There are different kinds of treatments, if at all. The interesting thing this dimension of psychopathy, which is so central to all of the other risk assessment schemes, does not seem to be that relevant in the assessment, the prediction of domestic violence, with one possible exception. Those of you who are familiar with the research know about the work of Jacobson and Gottman in, I believe, the 1980s. They identified the two kinds of batterers, the cobras and the pit bulls. The pit bulls just sort of explode and act out violently, while the cobras sort of lay in wait for their victims. The cobras seem to be a fairly small percentage. Very often there are combinations of the two. But perhaps the concept of the cobra bears some relationship to the concept of the psychopath.

So I come back to my initial point about the fact that in the domestic violence area, by not knowing the literature, by not having good research literature, by not having good normative data, we as mental health professionals are contributing to that pretextualism, the pretext that we are doing something meaningful, the pretext that we have competent evaluators, using well-normed instruments. We don't. We need to work on this.

Thank you very much.

Chapter 8
Trauma-Informed Custody Evaluations

G. Andrew H. Benjamin, J.D., Ph.D., A.B.P.P.

DR. JANET CUMMINGS: I know our next speaker is more than ready since he was even ready before the last speaker. We have heard quite a bit of talk about the bad custody evaluators, the people who are there to further their own agenda, to pad their own pocketbooks, or to make decisions that they think may be right, but based on wrong and faulty information and assumptions. Thank goodness there are exceptions out there who are also teaching others to do good custody evaluations, and one of those is our next speaker, Dr. Andrew Benjamin. He is both a lawyer and a family psychologist and is able to bring both dimensions into his evaluations and his ability to teach others to do competent and fair custody evaluations. Dr. Benjamin.

DR. BENJAMIN: Thank you so much.

Well, John (Dr. Caccavale) and David (Dr. Shapiro), I am here to say that in fact I do believe that we have a role in working with our families that are so split, and I think we can provide really good evidence for the lawyers and the jurists involved in these cases.

So let me start with standards for forensic evaluators conducting competent custody evaluations. But first of all, I am a graduate out of the University of Arizona. I am a licensed lawyer in the great state of Arizona. I am licensed to practice clinical psychology in Washington. And John's point about the APA guidelines is accurate. They are very general. But what we did with those guidelines is, we took those guidelines and actually crafted rules for psychologists. We drafted them and promulgated them through our licensing board in Washington, and those rules create standards of practice that are expected for competent custody evaluations. And I think that is really part of the answer that I hope you will take away today, is that we need to do a better job of educating and regulating the people who are involved in the process of conducting custody evaluations.

Now, you should wonder about my credibility. I would, for after listening to John and David, I would think, my God, why would anybody have a role in this kind of setting? Well, I have done more than 900 of these evaluations, and I have not had an ethics complaint. Let me say that again. More than 900 evaluations, high-conflict custody family law cases, the worst-of-the-worst cases coming out of King County in Seattle, Washington, to my program, and I have either conducted or supervised those cases and not had a complaint filed against me. I have trained now over 200 people to do these kinds of evaluations, and very few of those people have ever had an ethics complaint filed against them.

Now, this is a rare phenomenon, and it suggests that the protocol that we developed out of our program might have some valid and reliable aspects to it, because, if it didn't, you could count on complaints being filed against the practitioner. And judges and lawyers, I would ask that that should be one of the very first questions you find out when you think about the credibility of the psychological evidence that is being provided by some damn evaluator that is before you. Kids get hurt. If we do not rise to the standard of practices that I think need to exist throughout this country to perform competent psychological evaluations, comprehensive parent evaluations, in these case, kids will get hurt. My clients are the kids. That is what I teach my students and certainly what I do in my evaluations.

So these are the standards for forensic evaluators promulgated by the American Psychological Association:

- Maintain professional integrity by examining the issues at hand from all reasonable perspectives.
- Seek information that will differentially test plausible rival hypotheses.
- Engage in consultation if issues exceed competence.

You know, I did not give you the Washington standards. I would be more than happy to do that. I am also more than happy to volunteer to work with any lawyer, psychologist, or anybody else interested in creating standards within their jurisdiction whatever state you might be from or province, for that matter. And I have worked with the British Columbians, to create better standards.

We maintain professional credibility and our integrity in these cases by really adopting—and this is really important—a sensitivity to our own counter-transference. All of us have bias. And unless we are paying attention to how that bias might emerge within these cases, we will hurt kids. We also have to make sure that, as we go through this process, that we find ways of exacting a fair, organized approach. Now, I did qualitative research in developing the protocol on this. It has been published by the American Psychological Association. What I am going to talk about is how this protocol can be used to provide these trauma-informed custody case evaluations. This protocol is valid and reliable based upon thousands of hours of watching videotapes of both sets of parents—of mothers and fathers and children who have gone through this context. And what we did in changing the protocol is, whenever we found places within these evaluations where people felt surprised or people felt betrayed, where people felt abandoned or misunderstood, we would rethink that aspect of the protocol.

Bottom line: Unless people feel like they have been fairly treated, they are not going to change their behavior. They are not going to change their behavior. And these evaluations are a form of therapeutic jurisprudence, in my view. And we want to use the findings that emerge from these evaluations to help parents become better at parenting, certainly better at communicating with each other, if they can, if we can even get them to that point. In many instances, we can't. In many instances we have domestic violence in the case, and as that emerges, the data emerge, to corroborate that domestic violence has occurred, we can set up very straightforward recommendations that can help inform the lawyers how to get settlement out of that case, how to move that person into treatment to make sure that the kids and the mother, usually, get protected.

So we avoid the appearance of bias in large part by exacting the persona of being a very caring fair person, open to all the possibilities as the evaluation process unfolds, and we make sure that we seek information differentially across many different types of measures to test hypotheses. We do not rush to judgment on any particular finding.

So, all of our evaluations are court-ordered. We want the court involved in the process from the beginning. We want the court, in fact, to send questions that the court would like us to address. We would like the lawyers involved in those court-ordered evaluations to send questions that they want addressed. And then we get an elaborate questionnaire filled out by both of the parties. It is not a grammar test, and it includes a 28-domestic violence screening instrument. Where David talked about the various factors that are covered across all those measures, well, we want to find out if any of those behaviors have occurred. These evaluations, in my view, need to be driven by behavior. The best predictor of future behavior is past behavior. So we are checking for all aspects of potential control and domination that might have occurred within this relationship.

We also make sure that we are going to operationalize the parenting behaviors that need to change with very good concrete examples within the report, in a rich narrative report, so that the lawyers and judges can work out their counseling at law how to affect the party that they are representing or the party they are ruling for or against.

So they come in looking very interpersonally sensitive. These people that the judge is ordering to evaluation literally are the most interpersonally sensitive among all of us in this culture. So we want them to be because judges get to this place where they have got multiple allegations raised by both parties; we want to get to the place where we can provide good psychological evidence that the judges can rely upon regarding domestic violence, mental illness, substance abuse, economic strain, other kinds of issues such as educational deficits, or whatever. We are open to all questions that the jurists and lawyers might have.

I am going to go through the overview of our process. In particular, the most important aspect of our process is fairness. It is really important that throughout the process, no matter whether you are working with the batterer or the person who has been battered, your process seems fair. If you are going to use cognitive dissonance to get people to change, they need to have compelling data that emerge from this process. They need to feel like they have been heard. And so we avoid the surprises. We make sure that we are videotaping these evaluations, and under no circumstances are we letting our data enter the report unless it has been corroborated by multiple measures.

And we limit ex parte contact with the lawyers and judges involved in this context, in this business just to writing. We are happy to get written questions. We want everybody papered-up. We want to make sure again that the parties feel like they have been fairly treated. And by the time they get to us, more often than not, they haven't felt treated well. They have felt that their lawyer often has failed them. They have felt that other professionals within the system have failed them. They are pretty angry and pretty distrustful.

We screen out the inappropriate cases. If there is a criminal charge against any person within—that has been ordered into our process, we send a note back to court, and we ask the court to suspend the order until the criminal case has been prosecuted. Surprisingly, we still get cases where there has been a criminal charge. But, nevertheless, we wait until that evidence is in. We obtain the concrete referral questions that I talked about. We make sure that we send out a lengthy disclosure statement, laying out all the steps of our process. It is a five-page set of steps. We want people to know what we are going to be asking, how we are going to be asking them, and when we are going to be asking them. We do not want to surprise them. Right? We collect our fees upfront to avoid the multiple-relationship problem that John was talking about. And we have a sliding fee scale, and we will slide down to as low as $100 per party. And we make sure that we distribute the initial testing and consider those results to inform our structured interview. This is a very sensitive process.

So these are the kinds of questions that we will get besides our standard DV questions. We will get this back from both of the parties before we move into interviews. When we get to the interview, we make sure that we are finishing the disclosure process that occurs upfront. We do administer psychological testing—I will talk a little bit more about that in a bit—that the evaluation is allegation-driven. Any concern that a party has raised, we will investigate. We will evaluate. We will make sure that that concern is noted up front. We integrate the data immediately. For every hour we spent with the party, we spend an hour report-writing. And we make sure that we send out that report, the beginnings of that report, to the party that we have interviewed so that the facts can be checked. And if the facts come back and they are not right, what does that raise? It raises the hypothesis that biases occurred, that our counter-transference has affected our clinical judgment. And that, of course, leads to consultation and maybe even withdrawing from the evaluation. In some instances, we have had to do that.

We make sure that we are paying attention to what we know from the clinical research about judgment. Psychologists are very prone to clinical judgment errors, such as overreliance on memory, confirmatory and hindsight bias, and overreliance on unique data. These are the risks primarily that psychologists suffer from. That is one of the reasons why we always are writing contemporaneously with our interviews. We are making sure that we integrate those data immediately.

Our evaluations are broad-based and multi-measured. And this really borrows from the law because we know that the law really is an adversarial process. And when we have two parties that are able to share their concerns in a safe place, away from the threat of cross-examination, and that they are fully heard and fully understood around those concerns, we are going to get the best evidence. It is going to emerge. And we are going to use those multiple measures so that, as that evidence emerges, we do not rush to judgment based upon just one data point. We are looking for multiple-measure corroboration. If we do not get multiple measure corroboration, we are not arriving at any kind of finding about any evidence. We can honestly report back to the judge: We don't know. This allegation was raised, but we don't know. There wasn't enough evidence that emerged during the process to make a finding.

So a relevant cartoon the mother is putting up pictures of the father and says: "I put them up after the divorce so he knows his father is still part of his life." We get that kind of parent, and it also has something to do with psychological testing, because you know David is absolutely right: Our psychological testing at this point is not very refined. It does not really work for this population. What it can help with, though, is to generate hypotheses, and that is why we continue to do psychological testing.

We use standardized questions. This is something recommended by one of the very best papers in our field written by Emery et al. in 2005. And we are using those standardized questions to really draw out from the parties their concerns, and we are making sure, John, that there is no multiple relationships because we got the money upfront, and we know that the lawyers will continue to come back to us if they feel their parties have been fairly treated. They do. We do not have lawyers that are filing ethics complaints against us. And they would. And they do against our other colleagues, John.

I have got to say that parties going through this process are probably crazier than any other place except for Saturday night ER rooms in major metropolitan cities. If the judge is ordering them into evaluation, the judges are completely baffled. They do not send people to us lightly. And I really want to make sure that we address those parties' concerns, because they are real. They may be very interpersonally sensitive; that is true. But those concerns are real. They need to be addressed.

So we give releases of information upfront, and we make sure that anybody that has firsthand information about any of the allegations that the parties are concerned about will provide us a declaration, particularly nonprofessionals. We get declarations or affidavits because, under the laws of the particular jurisdiction, they swear they are not committing perjury. This is important. It is one of the ways of protecting the fairness of the process. So if somebody is willing to write an affidavit or declaration, we are willing to interview that person as an important collateral, particularly if they have got firsthand information.

One of the very best aspects of our evaluation process is observations with the parent and the child or children. They provide very rich data. And Dr. Walker is absolutely right. You know, kids will concentrate on the loving parts of their parents. And even though that is very, very true, there are baseline behaviors, parenting behaviors, that often do not emerge in these observations. And when they do not emerge, it helps inform our process.

We also have, despite those children focusing on the loving parts of their parents, parents engaging in very lamentable behavior that smacks of emotional abuse. Incredible, but it happens. On occasion, we will have flat-out startle responses going on as a parent reaches across a child for a toy and the kid startles as if about ready to be beaten, you know. So that is the kind of data that will emerge in these observations. With teenagers, of course, we are getting rich information about discipline, about chores, about the values of those parents, and how those values are meted out within the home context, very important information to incorporate as part of the multiple-measure corroboration.

We always use the legal factors to organize the psychological evidence. You know, our Judge Fields is right on target with this. I really feel as if the psychological evaluations have to be informed by the legal factors that the lawyers and judges are working with. If you organize the psychological evidence under those legal factors, those lawyers are much more able to reach settlement. It used to be that about 60% of our cases got settled. Towards the end of the program, the end of the last—I don't know—five, six years of the program, almost 99% of our cases settled. The lawyers can use the data if it is structured well. And we incorporated discussion about how the data really corroborate the limiting factors that have to occur. So if there is a finding about domestic violence, we are showing those data very clearly, with actual examples of what has happened in those DV cases, so that the judges can, or the lawyers can usually reach settlement around how that parent will have no contact and access with the kid until specific treatment occurs and specific protections are set in place and followed by the offending parent.

Often, you get so many data in this context that it could be confusing. It can lead to confusion. But, you know, if evaluators keep their eye on the ball, the data actually do begin to show the patterns that can lead to good findings. It is what Dr. Walker suggested in the beginning. Domestic violence is not a one-time incident. Mental health issues are not a one-time incident. Substance abuse is not a one-time incident. You know, you are going to have patterns that will cut across all areas of the life you are trying to understand. And those facts will emerge from the various measures.

When we move out of the observation process, this is the time where we write up our evaluation report, the rough draft of our entire evaluation report. We do this before we even interview any of the collaterals or look at any of the collateral documentation. Now, this is an aspect of our protocol that is controversial to many of my colleagues in psychology. I have to say that we do this because it is a matter of fairness. When we looked at the material beforehand, we were often accused of being prejudiced by the folks that came before us. And we did not want to be accused of being biased by other professionals who had been involved in this case. So we just avoided it altogether, and, frankly, it leads to a much more valid evaluation report, because the findings that emerge have been written up as a rough draft. Where there is multiple-measure corroboration, we have already identified that corroboration. Where there are rival hypotheses, we are beginning to see those emerge. And in many instances, some of our initial hypotheses have to be rejected because there has not been sufficient evidence that has emerged at that point. Nevertheless, we will test because of the collaterals that we are given, whether there was any firsthand information about some of those allegations which were not emerging with multiple-measure corroboration. And so that is a check on our evaluation process. Some of the best evidence is coming from firsthand observations, and, frankly, the very best evidence is an actual admission from the person involved in the behavior.

So we send a written summary whenever we conduct a collateral interview to the collateral the day we do the collateral interview. We make sure that there is a meeting of the minds around what we heard from the set of questions we have asked. And we interview particular people much later in the process, really at the very end, right before we interview the party in the closing interview—for instance, a paramour we would never, ever interview until right before we are giving the feedback to the party in our closing interview, because that paramour is likely to change her story. And if that paramour is a potential DV victim, we want to give her sufficient information right before we interview the person involved in domestic violence because, in most instances, we are now getting admissions from the batterer about his battering. It is a way of protecting his second paramour.

We reject material that does not bear directly on the allegations' collaterals. Professionals in particular are very chatty, and love to raise information that just is not relevant in light of the concerns raised by the parties and the questions raised by the lawyers and the judge in the case. And we do make sure again that we are paying particular attention to those issues that will lead us to be able to protect the children.

So this is the very toughest part of the process for most psychologists, and most of my colleagues wimp out. They are not meeting with the people they are evaluating. Now, you heard Dr. Walker say that she does. Bless her heart. She is a rarity. And I think it is so critically important that you lawyers and you judges make sure that this occurs when you are asking about an expert's methodology. Make sure that this is part of the process, in large part because, you know, by the time we get to the closing meeting, we have more than enough evidence at that point to go through with the party, and we should. We want to do that. We want to be fair and respective with this party, and, again, we want to close the door on a later complaint about that party being unfairly treated. And so we give that party, if they disagree with a particular finding, some additional time to submit other evidence that we may have missed.

Yes, we will get parties exasperated at us and dissatisfied with us. But what happens is we lay out each damning fact that has led to a particular finding one fact after the other. That cracks denial. That cracks the minimization that goes on in many of these cases. And parties come away again feeling respected and fairly treated. They may not like what has been found by them—about them, but when they admit to an aspect of the facts that have led to a finding. For instance, about domestic violence, we will ask for other information about the time that they thought was the worst domestic violence they perpetrated. And when we get those disclosures, that is cognitive dissonance. That person is going to be much more likely to change in batterer's treatment.

We meet with the lawyers and with the guardian *ad litem* (*GAL*) as a group, and we issue the final report at that point, and it is important on that they are permitted a follow-up conference if they want because they have not—we do not give them any chance to read the report. At that meeting we want those lawyers to really test our credibility by raising the concerns that they have and be able—without being really elaborately prepared. It works a little bit better. Lawyers spend less of their client's money that way too.

That's how we don't give our soul away, John. We don't.

I just want to say in closing that for any psychologist out there, if you are willing to conduct pro bono cases, we need you. The judges need you. I am happy to serve as a free consultant no matter what your jurisdiction is, and I will share all of my materials with you for free if you will do pro bono cases, and I will make sure that you will learn about the standards of practice that can result in fairer evaluations being conducted on people who desperately these kinds of evaluations.

Thank you very much for listening to me.

Chapter 9
Trauma-Informed Treatment for Traumatized Children

Ricky Greenwald, Psy.D.

DR. JANET CUMMINGS: Our next speaker is Ricky Greenwald, a clinical psychologist. He is a university professor and previously was Assistant Clinical Professor and Director of Training for the Child Trauma Program at Mt. Sinai School of Medicine. He was part of a project in Hawaii providing child and family mental health services via the public school system, and one of his major specialties is in the area of trauma, and he will be speaking to us on trauma-informed treatment for traumatized children. We have talked quite a bit about the trauma that children experience in abusive families and in family court hell, so join me in welcoming Dr. Ricky Greenwald, who will be talking to us about solutions for those children and their trauma.

DR. RICKY GREENWALD: Hello. I am Ricky Greenwald with the Child Trauma Institute. If you want to get a copy of these handouts or the related research, go to our website: www. childtrauma.com. You can send me an email from there: any questions, comments, complaints.

Here's the plan for the next half hour. I am going to talk briefly about the impact of the kinds of events we are so concerned about, such as domestic violence and abuse. So we are going to start off with a brief summary of the impact of exposure to traumatic events, and then I am going to tell you what to do about it from a psychotherapy point of view. I am going to spend a little time talking about some of the leading trauma resolution methods that are used within a systematic treatment approach and, finally, how the court can help support the child's treatment.

I want to just give you a summary of the types of symptoms and problem behaviors that can either be caused or made worse by trauma, broadly defined to include certainly the types of events we have been talking about, and there is a lot of research on Trauma Informed Treatment (TIF) to back this up.

- Greenwald (2003), before/after in residential tx for teens: 50% reduction incidence, all categories.
- Farkas et al (2010), controlled comparison to TAU with youth in care in Quebec: Reduced PTS and problem behavior.
- Greenwald et al (2012), before/after FTM ll-staff training in teen residential: 39% reduction of treatment time, 103% increase in positive discharge rate.
- Becker et al (2011), San Diego community center/ clinic demo project: 87% retention rate, with completers doing well.

We are not just here to talk about PTSD. We are here to talk about the impact of post-traumatic stress on children, and it's across the board. With the exception of a few apparently biologically-based things like autism, just about anything else you can get can be caused or made worse by trauma. So those of you who are in the psychotherapy field may be aware that there have been competing trends in psychotherapy for decades and decades. One trend has been what you might call diagnosis-specific treatment, which is, you got somebody with depression, you do the depression treatment; you got somebody with anxiety, you do the anxiety treatment; and there has been a whole body of research focused on that. That comes out of the medical model, which actually works sometimes in medicine, where if you make the right diagnosis, you can do the right treatment and sometimes cure the patient.

There are a couple of problems with the diagnosis-specific approach. One is that most of these diagnosis-specific treatments are developed in university laboratory studies where people are cherry-picked to have only that problem and nothing else, and we don't meet people like that in real life in clinical practice, and so what do you do when you have a diagnosis-specific treatment and you have somebody with two or three diagnoses and half of one or two others? Which one do you use? Can you have treatment fidelity? It's just a mess.

And then the other thing is that when you compare those to sham treatments or so-called placebos, yeah, they look great; but if you actually compare them to other legitimate treatment approaches, they are not necessarily any better, and so the other line of psychotherapy research has been what you might call the common-factors approach, which is—you have all heard of empathy, warmth, and positive regard—and there is quite a large body of research documenting that certain common factors in therapy are more predictive of whether the clients get better than what the therapist thinks he or she is doing, in terms of, "Oh, I'm psychodynamic," or "I'm a play therapist," or I'm this or I'm that. Right now, those two lines are coming together because the diagnosis-specific people are recognizing that it is not a realistic approach.

On the other hand, that doesn't mean that all treatments are equal. There are still features of treatments that make some more suited to certain types of clients, but what I'm going to present to you is a systematic treatment approach. Oh, there's another problem with the medical model I forgot to mention.

If you have a medical problem, like, say, a broken leg or a strep throat and the doctor says, "I know what's wrong with you and I can fix you," that's good news. You know, bring it on. But when the core of a traumatized child's problem is feeling damaged and feeling helpless and the doctor says, "I know what's wrong with you and I can fix you," that actually reinforces the problem. "Oh, I am damaged and I am helpless. I'm glad somebody can fix me because I'm helpless." So it turns out that the medical model is also not a good model from an attitude point of view. It doesn't put us in the right place to actually help our clients. By the way, I say "clients," or "customers." "Patients" are people who wait for the doctor, wait their turn for the doctor to cure them. That's where the word comes from—sitting on the bench, being patient. It turns out it's not constructive for trauma-informed psychotherapists to have "patients" because they don't need powerful people to fix them. They need to do it themselves. So I'm going to present to you a phased model of trauma-informed treatment that is also—rather than using the medical model of the doctor fixing the damaged, helpless patient—it's an empowerment model of the client fixing himself or herself.

The Fairytale Model

This is called "the fairytale model," and it starts out with, well, a story. Once upon a time, there was a kingdom, a little kingdom—there's kingdoms and queendoms everywhere—and in this kingdom people went to work, children went to school, some people went to church or temple or mosque, not everyone.

Sometimes people would get together and share food, play games, play music, tell a story. Most people got along, but not everyone, and that's the way things were until one day a dragon came. Now, this dragon didn't just set up shop in the middle of town. Dragons mostly hide out in dark places. But dragons get hungry. One day the dragon took a sheep from somebody's pasture. Another time, he took a dog right from somebody's front yard. Well, the parents told their children, "Don't go outside. I don't want you getting snatched by some dragon." But they found out that their children weren't very good at not going outside, so they stayed home to guard their children. And even people who didn't have children, they weren't up for going outside either. So as you can imagine, things really slowed down in this kingdom. When people did get together, you know what they talked about: "How come we got a dragon anyway? Other kingdoms don't get dragons. Why do we?" And they didn't know. And they wanted to know. So they tried to figure it out. Actually, one group of people, they had it figured out. They said, "You know, those people who don't go to church, God's mad at us. That's why the dragon is here." Well, another group of people had it figured out a little differently: "Those people in that church with all the loud singing and the clanging and banging, it's the noise. That's what brought the dragon."

This kingdom got a bad reputation. The people from the other kingdoms, well, they didn't know about the dragon, but they sure knew what was going on and they would talk. They would say, "You know, those people, they don't go to their jobs. The children don't go to school. They are all arguing all the time. They are mad at each other. Nobody gets along. They're messed up." And that's the way things were, until one day a knight in shining armor came long. Well, no armor, not really a knight, just some guy. But when he walked into the kingdom, they saw something in him, and they said, "You! You're the one who can slay a dragon for us," they said. "Me? Uh, I'm not exactly a dragon slayer. I think you got the wrong guy, but maybe you can help me. I've been walking a long way from kingdom to kingdom because there's this girl I'm in love with and I don't know where she lives." He pulled the picture out of his pocket. He passed it around. "Anybody seen her?" Well, they saw the picture and they said, "Hey, that's our princess. She lives here and she wants to get married to the one who slays the dragon." He said, "Well, in that case, I'm your man. Take me to your dragon." And they did.

They took him to the dark place where the dragon was sleeping, where he took a look. He said, "Yeah, uh, ah, ah, ah, I don't think so. It's big. It's strong. It's scaly. It breathes fire. Bad idea. Let's just forget the whole thing." "Nah," they said. "You can do it. We know you can. You can build up to it. We will help. We will give you a personal trainer, and remember the princess." "Oh, yeah. I'm in love with that princess. I don't know about this personal trainer thing, but we'll give it a try and see how it goes."

Well, they took him to the schoolyard where there was plenty of room to work out. They didn't have any equipment set up yet, but they wanted to get him started. Run laps. Okay? He was nervous about the dragon too. He had never run laps; pushups, but it was the same thing. He'd get started, hear a little noise, jump up, and look around. And he said, "Never mind the schoolyard. It's not going to work here."

On one edge of the kingdom where the forest started, there was a clearing, a big open space. One side of the clearing already had high trees. Around the rest of the clearing they started to build a fence. Everybody helped. People were cutting down trees for it, putting them up. Other people were cooking for the crew. Even the little kids, they would be bringing people water, carrying messages. Everybody helped. And before long, they had a high fence around the rest of the clearing. Then he really got to work.

He ran laps. He did pushups. He lifted weights, did all kinds of special exercises. Every day, the personal trainer pushed him just a little harder, added a pound here, a pound there. After a while he started looking pretty good. When they thought he was almost ready, they had a couple of athletic teenagers from the kingdom dress up like dragons to give him a little practice. Now, he didn't use a sword for them, just a stick, but he got to practice his dragon-fighting moves.

Finally the day came. He was ready. He faced the dragon. He fought it. He slew it. Well, he did get to marry the princess. He was happy about that. She was too. Lucky thing—you never know. But things didn't go back to exactly the way they were before. For one thing, they had a hero living there now they didn't used to have. The people from the other kingdom, now they are saying, "Wow! They got a dragon slayer. I wish we had one!" And in this kingdom everybody is walking a little taller. They knew they had all been part of it. Also, you know what they are talking about now: "How come we got a dragon anyway? Other kingdoms don't get dragons. I wonder if we are going to get another one?" And they didn't know, and they wanted to know. So they hired a consultant. The consultant came. She looked everywhere. She interviewed everyone. Finally, she called a meeting. She said: "You got two problems here. First of all, everybody throws their garbage in the dump. It is piled high with garbage. It stinks! For miles! That smell attracts dragons." So they decided they would do more recycling. Everybody had a compost in their own yard; better for the gardens anyway. No big stink. The second problem she told them about, she said, "The section of the kingdom where your farms are, it is just flat, flat, flat for miles. Dragons are lazy and you make it too easy for a dragon to just, shhhhhoop, cruise right in." So they planted clusters of apple trees all through that section. It wouldn't be impossible for a dragon to come, but with all those barricades, it wouldn't be so easy either.

Well, you can guess what happened next. After a while, they had a lot of apples. So every year in the fall, they had an apple festival. It was a big thing. People came from all the kingdoms for miles around, and they had apple pie contests and apple-throwing contests. They had "biggest apple" contests, "ugliest apple" contests. They had food, music, dancing, games, everything a good festival should have. And the big event on the Saturday night that everyone came to was the dragon-slaying contest. Now, they didn't have a real dragon so whoever won from the year before would be the dragon. The young people from all the kingdoms would be practicing and training for months for a chance to win this contest, which was a good thing because, well, for one thing, the contest was really fun. Also, if another dragon ever did come, they would be ready. Then, they did live more or less happily ever after. The end.

The Model of Psychotherapy

So that's the fairytale. How is that a model of psychotherapy? I can see the gears turning in your brain, after all, I am a psychologist, but let's spell it out a little. First of all, when you have a child in treatment, who is the knight in shining armor? The child. Sometimes they wish we were, but the real world does not work that way. Everybody has got to slay their own. Now, if I were a real doctor, my question would be, "What's wrong with you?" so I can make the right diagnosis and fix you. But, okay, if the child is the knight in shining armor, let's stick with this one for a minute, who is the kingdom? Just call it out—family and home and neighbors, school, doctors, court, etc. Everybody is the kingdom, yeah. And who is the personal trainer? That will be the therapist and later also the consultant. So I am not the hero; I am just the coach. And if I ask—if a coach asks the doctor's question, "What's wrong with you?" I am going to be coaching a loser. So a coach's question is a little different. "What have you got?" So when I train therapists, which is a lot of what I do—although I love it when judges invite me too—it's a lot of fun. But when I train therapists, I say, "You've got to find out good things about the client and about the kingdom." Because at the end of our evaluation, we've got to be able to say, "You've got what it takes to slay the dragon. This is the kingdom that's got what it takes to help you to do it, and here's the data that makes me say that." Because that's what we've got to work with. We also have to find out about the dragon, about the bad things that happened, because otherwise all we can say is what everybody else has been saying already, "This kingdom is messed up." So in this treatment approach, we've got to include trauma and lost history in our evaluation, and we have to find out about strengths and resources.

Then there is the matter of the princess. Nothing happens without the princess. We are going to be asking our clients to not only do personal training, which is quite a drag, but also to fight dragons, which really hurts. It's not going to happen unless there's a princess your client is so in love with that he is willing to go through all that. This tends to be what we're worst at as a community of psychotherapists and as a community of adults. We are really good at saying, "This is what the program is about. This is what your parents expect of you. This is what the judge wants." We are not so good at saying, "What do you want?" but that's an essential step in this treatment approach because, without it—well, I'll tell you what happens. I'm supervising a therapist and the therapist says, "You know, I feel like I am working harder than my client." And when I say that in a group of therapists, they all chuckle and nod their heads because we've all had that, and so I ask the therapist, "Okay, so what are your client's goals related to the treatment?" And the therapist says: So this is a phase model—and the—I don't have the English word. The main point of the phase—the essence of a phase model is not "do this intervention and then move on." It's "get this achieved and then move on." So whether it takes a minute or a month to get your client to say,

"This is what I care about and I'm willing to work for it," this is where we are until that's achieved.

Next up is the explanation we give to the client about how what happened to them a year ago or ten years ago is related to what happened to them yesterday that got them in trouble at school; and we talk about how the memories that were too overwhelming to digest got pushed behind the wall. It makes a sore spot. Now some little thing happens that hits the sore spot and it feels like a big thing and they have a strong reaction. That's the quick version. Because if they don't see the trauma history as part of the problem, they are not going to see addressing the trauma as part of the solution. And, indeed, this is one of the common factors found to lead to effective psychotherapy, is a shared understanding and agreement about what's going on with the client and what to do about it together. This is the foundation of the therapy alliance—we are working together on what we are agreeing on, right?

The Treatment Plan

And so here is the treatment plan that we use with every client in this treatment approach, child or adult, no matter what they think they are there for—substance abuse, depression, school failure, aggression—here's the treatment plan. Build a stronger fence around. Do your personal training. Slay the dragon.

And for those of you who are psychotherapists or who are familiar with the field, you will notice, with just a little thought, that this isn't instead of what therapists already do; this is just a way of organizing what therapists already do. So the next step is "fence around," because we understand that if clients are busy watching out for the dragon, if they don't feel safe and secure, they are not going to be able to concentrate on their personal training. So this is where we do case management, get basic needs met, try to ensure safety. You can see where this ties into everything else, right?

And, with teams, we also teach them to build their own fence by avoiding high-risk situations. How long does it take to build a good-enough fence? A week, a year—as long as it takes. Not to build a perfect fence—none of us have that—but at least a good enough one that the client is going to be able to concentrate on the next step.

Personal training—this is where we do all the self-management skills: communication, problem-solving, anger management, anxiety, etc. And not only are clients building up their coping skills, but they are also learning how to tolerate that sore-spot reaction, the overreaction of very strong feelings, for long enough to handle it the right way. So they are building up their skills and their strength, which is very important, because if you are going to be fighting dragons, you've got to be able to take the punch. When it's time to slay the dragon, we're still the personal trainer. We are the personal trainer all the way through. We are always adding a pound here, a pound there. We don't go for the biggest dragon in the pile. We start with the snake, some little thing that happened yesterday in school, just for practice, and then maybe a baby dragon until we're confident that our client can handle the bigger challenges.

Differing from Most Trauma Training

And this is a good time for me to mention that I have a beef with most trauma training in the world, because when you go for trauma training, you go for the sword. That's what the trainings are called: Eye Movement Desensitization and Reprocessing (EMDR) training, for example, or prolonged exposure training—or whatever it is—you go for the sword, the trauma resolution procedure. And I've been to these trainings, and they spend most of the time teaching you how to swing the sword, but they don't teach you how to be a personal trainer. They don't teach you all the steps. And so what we find across trauma resolution methods is that most people don't use it well enough, appropriately, or at all, because without being a good personal trainer, you are not in a position to help your clients slay the dragons.

So when you're getting training, make sure they teach the whole thing and not just how to swing the sword. And when you are referring, you want to ask the therapist a couple of questions. It's not enough to say, "Oh, yeah, I'm an expert"—everybody thinks they are an expert—but to make sure that they're really going through the steps. And this is just—there are a lot of phase models around. They are all a little different, but they are all essentially the same, so you ought to hear—even if you don't hear the fairytale jargon, you ought to be hearing these kinds of steps— helping the clients to understand what is going on and what to do about it: stabilization, skill building, trauma resolution. So what happens after the dragons are slain? The sore spot is down. Do the problems melt away? Quite often they do. It's pretty cool. And, just as often, they are reduced but they're still—you know, people have habits. They have life situations, personalities. So we often go back into another round of "fence around" and personal training. Now that the post-traumatic stress isn't driving the symptoms, we see how much farther we can get. When we've got as far as we can get, even then we don't simply say, "Great work. Have a good life!" We help clients to anticipate future challenges. Are there high risks coming up that can be avoided? For challenging situations that can't be avoided, can we get you ready with your coping skills? And if another traumatic event should happen or if you back-slide into your bad habits, can we at least have the dragon slayers ready so you can catch yourself and get back on track—you and your family—and catch yourself and get back on track before it goes really bad again.

So I'm just going to tell you that there's quite a lot of research. I mean, the phase model is the standard of care in trauma-informed treatment, and we've got some preliminary research on this particular model as a package—there we go—across a wide range of diagnoses with a number of challenging populations in foster care, residential treatment, and in impoverished urban neighborhoods where we are getting very high retention rates, kids engaging in the treatment, families engaging in the treatment, and kids getting better—very challenging kids. This isn't, you know—there are a lot of really good trauma therapists around that have never heard of this, so this isn't the only way to go. I like this particular model. I'm really giving it here as an example, but also I happen to like this particular model for a couple of reasons: One is, it has a story. So when I train people, it's not just a list of "Do this, then do that." It has meaning because you connect it to the story. Also, we have scripted interventions at each step so that this is actually a replicable treatment. It's not just a theory and then you watch somebody do it and you say, "No, that's not what I meant." You actually give them the words, and they can do it, and it works with their clients, because these words were developed in the field. So people can get the steps accomplished their own way or they can do it our way. So whether somebody is using this particular model, they should be doing something like this, I think.

The Swords

I want to focus a little more on the swords. The good news is, we have got some good swords now. Twenty years ago, the rap for trauma treatment is, "Okay. We have some good treatments, but they are a huge ordeal. You've got to go through the memory over and over again. We are getting 35% to 40% dropout rates because people get re-traumatized by the treatment"—back in the days when these treatments were called things like "implosion therapy" or "flooding"—and then you only get so much cure, and then we'll help you learn to cope with the rest of your symptoms with self-management skills and medications.

Well, now we're so good at what we do—not that we're so good, but we have better procedures now—that we can pretty much say, "You do the work and you're going to get there. You're going to heal. You're going to come out stronger than before," not 100%, but really very high success rates.

So I want to tell you a little more about some of the leading swords. First of all, they have a fair bit in common. All require the preliminary steps before you get to the sword. If your client isn't motivated and determined enough, stable enough, and strong enough, you shouldn't be slaying dragons. So whatever sword you are using, you have got to be doing the prep involved in the phase model.

Secondly, all the proven effective swords—that means the ones that have stood up to research—you have to actually face the memory and work your way through it. I use the term "digestion," but people have their own, you know, integrate process, whatever. You have got to work your way through it to get to the other side. None of the "magic wand" methods have been proven effective yet. That's a disappointment, but that's how it is. So, all the proven, effective ones—the client really does have to do the work—but among the proven, effective methods—as the pig famously said, "Some are more equal than others"—oh, yeah, that too, okay—in terms of the client's ability to withstand the procedure, the types of clients, types of presenting problems they work with, how quick they are, and how easy it is for therapists to learn.

Types of Treatments with Children

So I'm going to tell you about the ones that you're most likely to encounter with children. I just want to mention that I was in a training session where I worked with the same therapists over a number of weeks, and on the third day of training, which was the third weekend, one of the trainees came in talking about a new client she had had. This is a very New-York-City story from when I worked at Mt. Sinai. She had gotten an 8-year-old boy who had had a major traumatic event at age 6, had been going to therapy for two years once a week. Confidentiality. The mother brought the kid, picked him up, wrote the check, had no idea what was going on in the black box in the room. But after two years, nothing was getting better, and so she just finally decided to try a different therapist that happened to be taking my class. So this new therapist, in the very first meeting, said to the boy, "How much did you talk about the trauma with Dr. So-and-So?" And the boy said, "Oh, we never talked about that. She wasn't ready yet." [Laughter] Thank you. This is a true story, and I'm reasonably confident that that Dr. So-and-So represented herself as very experienced, goes to conferences, and really believes she knew what she was doing, but she wasn't using a sword, she was using a stick, and it doesn't get the job done.

So I want to tell you about some of the better swords that you are likely to encounter. One of them is play therapy, which can either be a sword or a stick, depending on how it's used. If you just sit back and let the kid play and make comments once in a while, the kid will feel comfortable, she will like you, but she won't get better—at least not usually. On the other hand, there are structured play methods where the child is guided to really work through the trauma memories—using monkeys and alligators and whatever's handy—to work through what happened, and that can be a sword.

Another one that has been widely disseminated lately is trauma-focused cognitive behavioral therapy (TFCBT), and in this method the child is guided to create a story book, literally a book, of the trauma memory, page by page. This works well.

It allows the therapist to be a good personal trainer, because if I don't think this client is ready to handle the heavy page yet, we'll start on another one, and as she digests that tangential piece, that makes her stronger to face the bigger stuff later. So it's a pretty nice system. It's relatively easy to learn. It's widely disseminated. It has had a very rough adaptation to community settings, so it tends to work well with single traumas with high-functioning kids and high-functioning families. But when you go to the community mental health centers, a few are managing to adapt it and make it work, but many are not using it very much and can't get kids to do it. Another issue with trauma-focused CBT is that it takes quite a number of sessions to get through a single traumatic memory, and if you've got a kid with a history of chronic trauma, it's going to be quite a long treatment.

This brings us to EMDR, which has also been widely disseminated, not so much a top-down thing based on funding like TFCBT, but really grass roots dissemination, with therapists flocking to workshops. This was, along with recovered memory, the other hot controversy in the mental health field in the 1990s, but it's controversy no more. It is now routinely listed in all the lit reviews as being among the top two or three treatments of choice for trauma, and there are a couple of med analyses: one submitted for publication that, for the first time based on a larger number of studies—which you get to do by waiting a couple of years since the last study—EMDR has now been found to be more effective than the other leading brands in direct comparisons, and in one that we are working on right now, it's also more efficient. This is kind of embarrassing, that a therapist like me would invent a statistic, but it's true. It is sort of a miles-per-gallon statistic for psycho-therapy, so we're doing a change-per-minute analysis, and EMDR is coming out more efficient than the other leading brands. The procedure in EMDR is: you ask the client to focus on the worst moment from the memory, move their eyes back and forth for a few—half a minute or so, report what came up, what they noticed. And whatever they say they noticed—"I'm getting more mad now," "I remember this other part of it"—whatever it is, the therapist says, "Concentrate on that now. Do another round." And it's a very strange process. It's almost like saying, "Go dream about that now." But clients can do it, children can do it, and it's way faster than other stuff. And it's good. So the problem with EMDR is that it's very complicated training. It's resource intensive. Even then, most therapists don't learn how to do it well enough to use it well. So everything's a mess. And—I want to just mention a couple of up-and-coming trauma treatments that I won't discuss now, but at least I want them on the page, that could be improvements in that they're both very efficient, very well tolerated by children, easier to learn and to do than EMDR. But I don't think we have enough research on these yet to take it to the bank.

Getting Better in the Family Court System

Changing gears one more time, I want to spend just a minute or two talking about how the family court system can help kids get better. Now, you know the old expression, "It takes a kingdom just to slay a dragon." That certainly applies here. And you might not believe me, but I actually didn't consult with any of the other speakers before I prepared my slides, but they saved me a lot of trouble here, because it turns out that what's good for children is also good for their healing and recovery. So let's go through these quickly.

You have got to keep children safe. You can't get over something that is still going on. And that also applies to contact, because contact that might look innocent from the outside, can feel very threatening to a child, especially one who has not yet recovered from what happened. That doesn't always mean there should never, ever again be contact, but as we've already gone over, it should be focused on what's good for the child.

As many have said, and which I strongly believe, you bring children into the world and your first obligation is to them; your second obligation is to yourself. So when we have a choice, we focus on the child's needs before anybody else's. The child's legal representative—this assumes that there is one, which I believe there should be in many cases—should advocate for the child's best interests. And I think we could have an interesting debate on whether that's what we should be doing or whether we should be talking about the child's wishes. This is how I see it, but I think it would be a very interesting debate.

And this hasn't been brought up yet, but I think most of us in the room are quite aware that the court is often used as a weapon by the abuser as an instrument of abuse to control, to coerce, to beat protective parents into submission, to exhaust them financially, etc. And even though the judicial guide to child safety in custody cases specifically goes over the kinds of remedies that judges are encouraged to use to prevent courts from being used as instruments of abuse, that guidance, I don't think, is being taken to heart often enough. But it would be very important, because when you hurt a child's protective parent, you are hurting the child, when you exhaust somebody financially, when you're harassing them, etc.

And that brings us to the issue of the non-offending parent. The goal here—again, I can go through this quickly because we've been talking about it all day and yesterday. When a child's safety has been imperiled, parents' rights are not paramount, child's rights are paramount, and we no longer should have a goal of trying to be fair to parents. When you abuse a child, you have forfeited that as a priority. So the goal is ensuring that the child at least has one good parent who is empowered to do the job. And when you have a parent who is empowered to be a good parent—

who has authority, who has security—that's good for the child. That makes the child more safe and secure and more able to do their work with their therapist. So, as a psychologist, in my opinion, courts can help parents by empowering the non-offending parent to say, "Hey! I protected you in court and this is what the court decided because I fought for you." I'm dealing with parents all the time who are tied up by the courts because these are the parents who are trying to follow the rules and the court says, "Don't talk to the kids about this." And then the child has a parent who, in the child's experience, isn't protecting him, and that's not good for children. Parents should be able to live their own life, live where they choose, where it's good for them, where it's good for their children. They should be able to use their own parental judgment and prerogative, and this is not new—thank you, everybody else; you saved me a lot of trouble—and if contact with the abuser has been stopped, it should ultimately be up to the parent—the protective parent, the custodial parent—to determine what's good for their child in this, as in anything else, because, otherwise, they remain at the mercy of the abuser and they live in fear until the child turns 18. That's not good for the parent and it's not good for the child.

So the good news is, if we can keep the kid safe, we can get him healed. And it is a great time to be a therapist. The bad news is, not everybody knows this stuff. That's why myself and many others are working as hard as we can to train people up, because we didn't learn this in graduate school, but it does work. It's pretty reliable.

So when we can keep kids safe, when we can empower their parent and support their relationship, their security and attachment with that parent, kids and parents will come out okay.

Thank you.

Chapter 10

Family Therapy with Children in Custody Litigation

G. Andrew H. Benjamin, J.D., Ph.D., ABPP

DR. JANET CUMMINGS: Welcome back Dr. Andrew Benjamin, who spoke about trauma-informed custody evaluations. He will now be speaking on family therapy with children in custody litigation. Dr. Andy Benjamin.

DR. BENJAMIN: I just love following Dr. Ricky Greenwald. Ricky, thank you. You have made my job so much easier.

I'm going to be talking in particular about this notion of how therapy, believe it or not, can be helpful to the various players in the system. Not just the kids. Certainly the kids—they are the first folks that we are worried about and we want to help—but also the judges who, as I mentioned earlier today, have their courts flooded with pro se or pro per clients that have alleged many allegations and the judges don't know what to do with them. Of course, we have attorneys in the system. And, by the way, I am looking for a Maricopa lawyer who can provide pro bono work in a very important case here in this county. If I can have some volunteers, I would appreciate it, or if you know of some people who would engage in these kinds of cases, please let me know about it. I will make the request at the end of the talk too. But attorneys often will get involved in these cases later in the process, even though the pro se has come forward and moved the case as far as she or he can. Generally, at some point attorneys become involved.

And then, of course, you have the family members themselves and the mental health professionals involved in this process. So as Judge Wren says, therapeutic jurisprudence has a place within our legal system. It sure does. And this is a model of therapeutic jurisprudence. I've drawn upon a therapeutic jurisprudence model to flush out how to bring these two systems of mental health and justice together in ways that will work to protect kids, and that's hard. You've heard how hard it has been, but I think we have got a really good model going. So test this as we proceed.

I also think that for attorneys, who sometimes engage in this approach of family therapy; it provides them with some of the best evidence to protect the kids and the parent who is trying to protect the kids. And we also know that—and I think we've heard this repeatedly—and this is one of the reasons why I love Ricky's presentation. He is evidence-based research. Well, we need to do evidence-based research, and I am happy to report that I have got colleagues in Travis County—that's Austin, Texas—and we will be doing a treatment outcome approach using this model that I am going to talk about today. So the goals of family therapy with parents, the approach that we use, is to really make sure that the kids have a way of working through their parents' conflict and not getting caught up in it. And, generally, we are not talking about the worst-of-the-worst cases here that get referred into our program. We are talking about that realm within the 70% to 80%. So we've got some allegations that have been raised, no battering allegations generally, no substance abuse allegations, but, man, there are lots of questions about whether one parent is a good parent or not. And those issues may touch upon domestic violence, may touch upon substance abuse, but there is no good evidence that has been filed within the petitions. So we are focusing then on trying to build a therapeutic relationship with the child as one of the goals of this approach and also teaching the child how to depend upon the healthy adults around them, including grandparents, as part of our approach. For family therapy with parents, we want to increase the power balance. Generally, these cases come in with at least one parent significantly impaired. We want to make sure that we teach how they can disengage from conflict and their previous marital roles, and we want to increase the parenting and communication skills, resolve disputes, and also reduce the litigation.

Now, Ricky has suggested that—we haven't mentioned this much; but, in fact, it is the actual truth—we have abuse of use of litigation in this culture, and one of the ways that good people are ground down is having to respond to motions and petitions over and over and over again. We stop that with this process.

So, you know, when parents are at war with one another, kids get hurt. So this is an approach where we can actually help the parents stand down and definitely get the kids out of the middle. And, again, test that thought as we move along.

Really, as Toby Kleinman said, the kids' interests have to come first, and we put the kids' interests first. These citizen children need to be safe and secure. This is an approach that satisfies that requirement. We need to make sure also, and I think this is important, that the family therapist is not drawn into the conflict and, in effect, used and spat out by the justice system. So this approach satisfies that concern.

We also want to make sure that we stop the sabotaging that goes on between parents that are in that kind of band up to about 80%. It is not that we haven't seen any domestic violence, but, man, it is emotionally abusive what goes on, lots of that, back and forth. And typically one party, and it is usually the male, has economic control and domination in the relationship, and the sabotaging often works through those realms. So it is so important in this kind of case, and I will go through these phases in just a little bit, that the therapeutic alliance is still first for the child, definitely with both of the parties.

Whoops, here we go again. You heard this before. This is the key factor in making sure that you hold that therapeutic alliance. It's all about fairness. If either of the parents feels as if you are hunting them down, you will be fired. Now, we actually have set up this process so that it is very difficult for either or both parents to fire you; in fact, both parents have to agree to fire you before the mental health professional stands down. We also make sure—and this is really pivotal and I want to stress this—in these kinds of cases that we use email and texts for all parent interactions when they come into our family therapy system; no more in-person and phone contact. How come? We want to produce the best evidence. And when the evidence goes in writing, we can help people really focus upon their values and making sure they have acted congruently with their values. And we don't want to surprise people. So if we feed them back their words and we process their exact words using something called cognitive behavioral system and analytical psychotherapy—it is an evidence-based treatment too—we can get people to recognize that they are engaging in distorted thinking and move them towards healthier thinking and definitely healthier behavior.

Overview of PETP's Family Therapy Process

Phase One: Pre-evaluation Procedures

We don't do criminal cases, right? Somebody is convicted or there is a criminal charge, unh-unh, it's not ready for our process. No way. We won't get involved. And if there is a conviction, we don't get involved. I have talked about that earlier today. We distribute the steps of our process. We've got disclosure forms in the stipulation. Whoops. What's a stipulation? It is a term of art. The lawyers know about it. It is a contract. The parties agree up front when they sign this contract—after reviewing it, having plenty of opportunity to review it with their legal advisors and their mental health professionals and anybody else they want to review it with—they agree to many things, but there are three really important aspects of the stipulation. First, they can't fire me. They both have to agree to fire me before I can be fired. Second, if we get to an impasse and I can't use psychotherapy to come up with a good decision around their children, then they have to go into mandatory arbitration. I will talk about that more a little bit later. And, third—and this is really kind of another critical aspect of the stipulation—if they need specific individual treatment, for, let's say, an emerging substance abuse disorder or, in fact, somebody engages in an act of violence. We stop the process and they go take care of that in individual treatment, and the contact and access with the kid is removed during that period of treatment until we know that that parent is stabilized and that the protections built in around the contact and access with the kid so that that kid can't be hurt if the party does, for whatever reason, become destabilized. We obtain concrete referral questions. If there are attorneys involved or a judge involved, we make sure we collect the first advance fee up front.

We maintain a retainer of at least three hours' worth of work throughout the case and people pay as they go, and we charge, by the way, for the emails. Now, even if we are working with indigent cases, we still charge a little bit of money—a little bit of money—because otherwise we get too many emails and too many texts. Okay? So just a little bit of money, and we have a sliding scale that goes down to like less than a dollar per email so we can work out a financial arrangement that makes sense. And then we distribute allegations and issue a response. So, even if there has been a parent evaluation done by a reputable custody evaluator, that's great. I want, you know, the worst and the last two instances of each concern that the parent has when going into this process, and we want to know about those concerns right up front. We want to understand them from the parents' point of view, and I want to make sure that the parent feels validated about what those concerns are. This is about building a therapeutic alliance. It's about the common factors that Ricky suggested that are so critical in conducting good therapy.

Phase Two: Interview Parents Separately

So, yeah. So we do get lots of clarification to be very clear about what the parents have in the way of treatment needs. And we want to make sure right up front that people understand that they have waived really substantive rights, their signing that stipulation. It means they can't go to court. It means that they can't wait in a queue for six months to two years while lawyers are racking up legal fees responding to motions. It means that, with the mandatory arbitration process, resolution will happen within a week to two weeks, based upon the evidence, the email records, the texts that the parties provide to the arbitrator, victims' rights lawyers. Three victims' rights lawyers that have excellent reputations within the communities are nominated and put in the stipulation. They can choose among any of those three people. Whoever is available first is generally what I recommend. They get immediate resolution around any impasse. And we interview them and we are focus-driven during the interview so that we, at the end of this process, can say to them, "We've got a lot of work here. A part of what we want to do is make sure this work follows and is congruent with your values. This isn't about making you another Andy Benjamin. I want to know what your spiritual values are. I would like to know your nurturing values, what your values around children-focused parenting are, what your communication, what your sending and receiving values are, what your ethics are. I want those out in simple, declarative statements so that when we bump up against the tough issues, we can work through the CBASP process, the Cognitive Behavioral System of Analytical Psychotherapy, CBASP process, through your values to get to solutions. We are not going to hang out, you know, in feelings. We are going to work with behavior and your thoughts and we are going to move this process forward so that you feel empowered, because you are acting congruently with your values."

Phase Three: Observation of Parents Separately

So the next step is to do observations with each parent and child or children separately and, of course, depending upon the allegations, we'll structure the observation so we get a good sample of those realms in which the problematic behaviors between the parent and child might emerge; and I want a good sample of that behavior. And I also want the child to see me observing their parent and the child, or children, so that I have some credibility with that child, because I am going to build an individual relationship with that child through play and using the CBASP process while within play with the child.

Phase Four: Report Findings to Parties

And we don't stop. If the parent feels they need two or three sessions of parent-child observation to get a fair sampling of behavior, great, no problem; but I will give direct feedback about emerging parenting deficits that are clear from the sample that I have obtained, and maybe it will be added to the list of behaviors that we need to take care of at some point in the treatment of that child and parent. We will report those findings to the parties separately, and we will make sure that we frame the changes that they need to integrate by using the language of the parents' values. I have to say, that unless people feel as if they are understood and there are aspects of themselves that are powerful and strong and resilient, they won't change. Ricky's got that right. And I work through, really, their values—the best of what they have to offer—in order to get the changes to occur.

So, you know, Dr. Newberger mentioned this, but values really reflect upon character and decision-making. That's why I make such a big deal about values. But I also want to use the client's frame as much as I can in order to help that person see their way back to healthy relations. So we proceed with treatment and, not surprisingly, we use child play treatment. Ricky described it a little bit, but we really depend upon the common factors and resilience of the child, and we make sure that we are phasing the treatment and we are not pushing the child into processing whatever trauma the child has experienced until the child is ready. God, I hope that no child is going to say, "I wasn't ready," but, nevertheless, we are depending upon the play to really recognize whether we are at the point where we can cross into a good processing of the trauma. In many instances, our clients haven't had the kind of trauma that Ricky's clients have had. We are working with parties that are much less disturbed, I think, than the children of the parties that Ricky has worked with. So that makes it a little bit easier.

Nevertheless, we are prepared to work with even significant trauma, and, on occasion, we have.

Phase Five: Proceed with Treatment

I have to say, it's really about the parents. That's where the treatment really happens. It's really about the parents. And most of the kids are so wonderfully resilient and they move much faster than their parents do. But we will see parents relapse into their communication deficits. We will see parents engage in parenting behavior that is so lamentable and in violation of their values, and that's what we process. And we practice how to do it differently.

Now, I am a mandatory reporter. People know about that. If we get anything that is child abuse, the process stops. No coercion, right? Absolutely no coercion. The process stops. I declare an impasse, and, not surprisingly, we are in noncompliance of the treatment plan. People have agreed up front that they are not going to engage in partner violence, intimate partner violence, alcohol and drug abuse, denial of contact and access of the children. Those are the three big ones in our cases, and we expect people to hold to those promises that they made in the stipulation. So if it gets violated, we, of course, file mandatory—or we ask one of the parties to file for mandatory arbitration, and the written record of email and text exchanges around the lamentable behavior will be the evidence that will be presented to the arbitrator. Now, we also, if there is child abuse—we haven't had to do this too often, thank God—but if there is child abuse we will do a structured interview. I did a great article about a wonderful, structured interview that is highly valid and reliable. It is out there in the literature. I would urge all mental health professionals to take a look at that article. In that structured interview, we will write it out verbatim and that will be emailed out to the parties. That will be part of the record that gets before the arbitrator. Now, note that I am worried about mental health professionals getting burnt by the system, right? So part of the stipulation is, you can't call me as a fact witness, and you want an expert, you've got to go find somebody else to serve as your expert witness because I'm really only a fact witness, and when you sign the stipulation, you agreed that the only information that will be available is what is in the written record of the email and text. That's all you get. And it is done strategically because I don't want the kid to lose another healthy adult, right? This prevents my being viewed as a bad guy because I'm not making the decision about whether somebody has engaged in the lamentable behavior or not. That's the arbitrator's decision based upon that written record. The arbitrator will make a pretty quick decision. This is very effective for the following reason.

Phase Six: Impasse an Immediate Arbitration from Psychologically-Minded Lawyer

I don't wait. Instead, when it goes to mandatory arbitration, they have agreed in the stipulation that the person who files the arbitration has to put up the retainer for both parties. This prevents the abusive use of litigation. And unless the legal position is significantly improved, the person who files for the arbitration has to pay the whole cost. But not to fear. You know, in the few arbitrations that have gone through based upon the impasses that have been declared, they are coming out the way they should because the written record leads the arbitrator to the right decision. And we've got, remember, three victims' rights lawyers that we have named as arbitrators. So they are psychologically minded by nature and they understand the issues that typically are faced by family law court cases. So this is a very important part of their stipulation, and I would urge that—and I am happy to make the stipulation available to everybody—and I would urge that this be included because we don't want abuse of use of litigation being run. And that has happened in the earlier stages of this program, and I cut it off by engaging in this kind of behavior.

In particular, I have a treatment manual that I am willing to give out free that John Carr wrote, one of my mentors, and he has presented it at the APA convention back in '97. We have basic baseline behaviors that we expect, parenting behaviors that we expect, that Eyberg & Bogg set out in that article. I strongly recommend that article. It is a great article. And, of course, I am depending upon "The Theory of Cognitive Dissonance." This great Festinger article is wonderful. That's why we use people's values, why we get them to commit, to stay congruent with their values. That's why we work with people through the values. And George Kelly, of course, talked about that aspect, and then the McCullough article is about CBASP training.

And I think that is it. There we go. Thanks so much, you all.

References:

1. Carr, J.E. (1997). Cognitive-Behavioral Analysis System of Psychotherapy (CBASP). Paper presented at the APA Annual Convention, August 15, 1997.

2. Eyberg, S. & Bogg, S. (1989). Parent training for oppositional preschoolers. In C.E. & J.M.

3. Briesmeister (Eds.), (1998). *Handbook of Parent Training: Parents as Co-Therapist for Children's Behavioral Problems.* New York: Wiley.

Chapter 11

Trauma-Informed Family Court: Lessons Learned from Mental Health Court

Hon. Ginger Lerner-Wren

DR. JANET CUMMINGS: The next keynote speaker is the Honorable Ginger Lerner-Wren. Judge Lerner-Wren innovated the first mental health court in the United States in Broward County, Florida, and Congress has since used this as a model for federal legislation in 2000, creating mental health courts across the United States. I have actually had the opportunity to be in mental health court a handful of times as a clinical psychologist and have found it to work very, very well. So thank you for your innovation. I had not connected that to you until this conference, but I am very impressed by what you have done with what I have seen.

Judge Lerner-Wren ran her courtroom in a trauma-informed manner and was able to encourage people with mental health issues to take charge of their lives to find help in healing rather than just behaving in a punitive way toward them. She was one of the commissioners chosen to be on the George W. Bush President's New Freedom Mental Health Commission in 2002. As an aside, there have been only two President's Mental Health Commissions in U.S. history: the first by President Jimmy Carter and the second by President George W. Bush. So it is a rare distinction to have served on one of them. Here today we have two former President's Commission members: my father who served on the first and Judge Wren who served on the second.

Now, I am told that before I call Judge Lerner-Wren to the platform, I need to yield to Dr. Lenore Walker, for some reason which they won't tell me about.

DR. WALKER: Good morning, good morning, Ladies and Gentlemen. Thank you so much for joining with us this morning. We are going to help celebrate the launch of the Cummings County's newest problem-solving court, a child-centered family court, here in Cummings County. Please join with me in welcoming our first speaker, Judge Ginger Lerner-Wren.

JUDGE LERNER-WREN: Thank you. It is a great day in Cummings County, for as announced, the opening of the first ever child-centered problem-solving therapeutically oriented family court, specifically designed to protect the health, safety, and wellbeing of all of Cummings children and families coming under the jurisdiction of our family court system.

I want to personally take this opportunity to thank the Cummings family for hosting this morning's festivities and thank our courageous community, its stakeholders who served in our Cummings Problem-Solving Family Court Taskforce, distinguished members of our judiciary, elected officials, child health practitioners, advocates, and our distinguished guests.

I specifically want to thank members of the press and media for being here this morning to cover our community's innovative launch. I know, it's great. Where is our applause sign? Come on. We worked hard for this. This is a big, bold move. [Audience applause].

Before I talk specifically about our new court, I would like to share with you how we got to this day. On March 17, 2012, now to always go down in history as a historic conference. You remember, the broken family court system conference held on St. Patrick's Day. Come on. Yes, yes!

At this conference, as you recall, there was, it's true, an impassioned and chilling plea that was made by one of the conference attendees that we need to find a creative and innovative solution for our family court system, which, quite frankly, was losing integrity and public confidence. There was a perception that in fact our court processes were worsening victimization. The perceived problems, as we have come to know, that first of all our courts lack consistency in their use and reliance on court evaluations. This ultimately had a very detrimental impact to our court rulings, fact-finding, and also for all of our child abuse and domestic violence safety issues involving our children. The public confidence and trust were also being seriously eroded due to the fact that our courts lacked recordkeeping and transcripts of hearings by the courts that would effectively protect the pursuit of due process appeals. It also had a serious lack of integration of evidence-based research through and integrated into our court proceedings.

The court also began to have a reputation of really not appreciating or understanding the culture of victimization generally where child abuse and/or domestic violence was being alleged or was indicated. How did our community get ready to change? Thanks to the leadership of our family court administrative judge who listened to that impassioned plea—and here she is. She is coming in. A round of applause.

Thank you, Judge Fields, for your bold and courageous leadership because within 10 days of that conference and that impassioned plea, you went ahead and you used your judicial authority and you assembled a taskforce, a broad-based cross-section of our community stakeholders, to come together to find creative solutions to the problems that our broken family law courts were facing, and we knew what the main thrust of our goal was going to be. We were going to keep a strong focus on protecting the physical and psychological safety of our children of Cummings County. [Applause]. Excellent.

A diverse group of community stakeholders shared the concerns, and we got together, and we met and we met and we debated and we talked, and let me tell you something: Those debates got a little tense. Has anyone ever tried to reach consensus with Dr. John Caccavale, really?

But, finally, with the amazing Judge Fields leading, consensus was reached. Finally after months of meeting, the Cummings Child-Centered Trauma-Informed Family Court was born, and Drs. Benjamin and Greenwald graciously, as part of our team, agreed that they would step up to the plate and oversee the standards review committee on trauma-based evaluations and develop mental health interventions criteria to protect our children.

Dr. Shapiro graciously agreed to draft a judicial bench book and conduct trainings along with the distinguished Dr. Walker. Thank you, Dr. Walker. Thank you, Dr. Shapiro. And most important—and most important—thank you, Judge. So you are still leading. You are still leading.

And most important is Toby Kleinman, our "pit bull." Boy, when you tell her to seek the money, it doesn't have to be St. Patrick's Day, but she brings in the green. Our little bold experiment will be collaboratively funded by the National Association on Domestic Violence, the McArthur Foundation, and the Annie Casey Foundation. Give Toby Kleinman a hand. Couldn't do it without her.

And now to the court's mission. The mission of this court is simple: to take a problem-solving and therapeutic public safety and accountability approach to court process, where the court will take a multilevel and strategic approach so, where appropriate, the court will strive to be healing and restorative to families and the children through the application of therapeutic jurisprudence. In this regard, the court will produce an engaging and entertaining educational video produced by the award-winning filmmaker, Garland Waller—that's right—explaining the goals, mission, and unique services to be provided by our court. Therapeutic jurisprudence and how we will become a trauma-informed court will be done and offered to our family court bench and bar through regular trainings and no longer will family court be the experience from purgatory, also known as hell.

And we will ensure that every person appearing before this court understands the goals, missions, and objectives of our court process. The safety of our children is paramount to everything, and the court will establish emergency court intervention procedures as well as implementation of specialized risk management tools as developed and reviewed by the esteemed, distinguished, cute, Dr. David Shapiro.

The court will also identify through risk assessment screenings which cases present risk, and we will develop an accountability and safety plan for each family which will be filed with our local sheriff's office.

The court will be multi-systemic, as you can see, and collaborative. The court will collaborate with the Cummings Sheriff's Department to develop a specialized taskforce to assist in developing public safety strategies specifically designed to protect those families in the Cummings Family Court that are in high conflict or are families at risk. And also we will engage our local school administrators to assist in court process in terms of ensuring that our children court-involved are doing well in school, that they are not acting out with behavioral problems, that they are not being subject to expulsion or to entering into the juvenile justice detention—juvenile justice court system. So their involvement, their engagement, through their monitoring and offering of additional services is going to be a very big collaborative plus for our community.

The Cummings Child-Centered Family Court again will provide collaborative services to our families in a culturally competent way, recognizing that laws and the restructuring of the emotional, financial, and social aspects of family is often complicated and stressful.

In conclusion, our goal, through using evidence-based approaches, through data collection, and outcome measurements that are objective and reliable, we will seek to find out what works and where to direct our scarce resource. We understand the connection between disparities of wealth and what happens to children exposed to adverse childhood traumatic events, also known as the ACE study. There are those of you who are familiar with the ACE study and many other authoritative research regarding the connection of trauma and serious social problems. We understand the consequences of unresolved victimization, whether through domestic violence, substance abuse, or physical violence, and through the application of therapeutic jurisprudence and procedural justice principles, all litigants, including children, will be provided a voice, and their civil and legal rights will be protected as well.

And for those children that need to be offered the opportunity for court-appointed counsel *ad litem* specifically to represent the children's interests before the court, I am so proud to announce that the Cummings Law School has agreed to establish a clinical program of third-year law students just to support this effort for our children's legal rights.

Thank you.

Chapter 12

Understanding, Interpreting, and Addressing the Unbelievable in Men's Character and Behavior

Eli Newberger, M.D.

DR. JANET CUMMINGS: Dr. Eli Newberger is a pediatrician and faculty member of the Harvard Medical School. He was founder and medical director of the Child Protection Program, and even though he is now retired from Boston Children's Hospital's Harvard Clinic (1970 to 2000), he continues working as a consultant around the world on the rights of children. His perspective as a medical doctor on the character and behavior of men is insightful, highly unique, and important in the understanding of the struggles in the family court system. So please welcome Dr. Eli Newberger.

DR. NEWBERGER: Thank you very much. Some people may not have heard that Janet introduced me as the only physician on the various panels in the course of the conference and thus I must bring a kind of original perspective. I think I am going to bring something of a different perspective and different concept than other people, but it does make me mindful of a wise critical comment made by a Supreme Court Justice, likely someone who came from the Harvard faculty. And incidentally, for what little it is worth, I am still active at the Harvard Medical School as a faculty member, and I still have an appointment to Children's Hospital even though I have retired from the clinic. Felix Frankfurter was the distinguished Supreme Court jurist who wrote the introduction to his Harvard colleague, Alfred North Whitehead's book called *The Aims of Education* (1947 Edition). Frankfurter commented on one of the principal thrusts of Whitehead's argument about enriching education in the post-World War II era by nurturing the educational process by a variety of disciplines, as well as insights and work from the arts. And, indeed, when I was in grade school at the age of 10 in 1951, our elementary school had a full kit of band instruments. That was the first time I had a tuba in my hand, and this transformed my life. In fact, I met my wife, Carolyn, on the way to a jazz gig where I was playing tuba, and the leader of the band coaxed me into playing this freebie job on the tuba with the lure of fixing me up a date from Sarah Lawrence College, and that is Carolyn right over there. The tuba has been very important to me. I would not have had a tuba in my hand had it not been for this philosophy of education.

But Whitehead had a very serious comment in this introduction to the *Aims of Education*. He commented that there were risks in what was claimed to be the cross-fertilization in the educational process by the inputs from these various disciplines. And Frankfurter went on to warn about the possibility of the cross-sterilization of the disciplines, where doubt in one field would be resolved by resorting to a dubious truth in another. And in this domain of practice, we not infrequently see this occur. And I want just briefly to give you a critical preview of one salient event in the movie that we will see by Garland Waller, who is not only a filmmaker, but also Professor of Communications at Boston University.

In this story of Polly Ann Collins, who took flight to, and got asylum for herself and her children in the Netherlands, the judge in Minnesota who assigned the custody of her children to her abusive husband did so because of a psychologist's suggestion that this mother was a perpetrator of Munchausen Syndrome by Proxy and had sought evaluations and consultations from a variety of people, including my colleagues and me at Children's Hospital in Boston. Many of these had found, as we did, that these children had been seriously abused, with physical examination artifacts of abuse. So there was a dubious truth that if you organized the data in a certain way as he could deny the abuse and exercise what, in most of our views, would be a misogynistic reconstruction of the data. And we see this with parental alienation syndrome, and not infrequently in the sense that particular individuals will be able to offer a formulation in a situation where the court has doubt.

So, I mention this as the physician in this group, and as Janet said, the only one on the panel, from whom of course you can expect nothing but the unvarnished God's truth (tongue-in-cheek). So you have to take everything that I say with a grain of salt. Yes, there is the need for accurate diagnosis.

Now, my task is to talk about the depredations of men and to give you some tools to understand these. And as I look at the behavior of men and the astounding things that they do to children and women, which not infrequently confuse the court and challenge the court's and others' abilities to actually look at what is alleged as reality, I think that we neglect at our peril our own biology. So I want, in the course of this talk, to talk about some essential gender differences in human development and human behavior that I believe are very useful for us to understand.

Just in Walking into this Room

And I want to begin by calling your attention to your coming into this room this morning and looking around the room at men and women as your colleagues, people whom you may know and probably most whom you do not know. And if you think about your responses and feelings as you walked into the room, for many of us guys, we come in and we look at those other men, and our first thought may be, Can I take those guys or will I be subordinated in the event of a physical confrontation? The women laugh, "You do?" Can we really be like this? Well, actually, there was even a little contretemps about who came next after the first talk this afternoon among guys, if you will, jockeying in a playful way for position about who had priority at the lectern, the position of greatest authority in the room. Isn't this interesting?

When women come into this room, you look around at the other women in the room and you are not, for the most part, concerned about the possibility of a physical confrontation and your risk of subordination. Rather you look at the other women and wonder, am I going to receive a positive reception? Will there be people there for me? Will I find friends? Or am I going to be in some way marginalized and not accepted?

Well, what is going on here? Well, it has to do, if you accept what I say as valid, with our evolutionary heritage as males and females; indeed, how our brains are structured and how the cells and organs of our bodies respond to the hormones that course through our brains. And so now I want to give you a little bit of a lesson in neural anatomy, which will also pick up an extremely important point that Attorney Toby Kleinman made, the first time in these sessions when the concept of post-traumatic stress disorder was raised. It is very timely, because there is an unfolding body of research on PTSD that is—that analogizes to what I am going to say about gender. It feels appropriate to mention that as well, because it has some explanatory power for organizing the data of some of what we see in male and female behavior.

Our Biology Is Different: The Gerb Study

But I want to first just talk a little bit about anatomy. Our brains have, in distinction to the lower primates, an enormous number of cells and millions and millions of connections among those cells in the outer parts of our brain, the cortex, as it is called; "cortex" in Latin meaning "bark," meaning as in bark of the tree. And it is in the frontal cortex that we human beings uniquely have the ability to think about contingent possibilities and to take, when needed, decisive action, integrating memory, emotion, sensory inputs of all kinds as we look forward. As you can see from the information about me in the program, I have written a book called *The Men They Will Become, The Nature and Nurture of the Male Character.* And I was concerned as a physician and an authority, to be able to locate the things in male development that uniquely had to do with our propensities to make decisions at the gloral nexus, where we need to recognize and to reconcile our impulses and our desires against the needs and rights of others. This is how I define character. It is how most people define character. It manifests itself in the behavioral choices that we make throughout our lives. And, indeed, arguably it is how we judge character, and, indeed, for very many of us, we like to think that this is one of the things that we are doing in our practice on child abuse and domestic violence.

Well, there are more primitive portions of the brain that have to do with our animal origins, so there is a hindbrain. There are centers beneath the tentorium of the brain, the dense fibrous lining that separates the cerebral structures from the cerebellum.

The lower ones have to do with respiration regulation, with maintaining your heart, and connects to our cranial nerves, where we are able to sense feelings as well as sense smells and vision. These transmit to the upper portions of our brain through the midbrain these certain essential sensory inputs that we need in order to organize our experience and to move forward in life.

In PTSD, for example, the contemporary research demonstrates that there are impacts of traumatic experience. Indeed PTSD is not just something of a traumatic nature that happens to you, but sometimes, if not quite frequently, the trauma has something to do with what you witness happening to someone else in the theaters of war such as in Iraq and Afghanistan. Something that happens to someone whom you deeply care about—for example, a buddy in war whom you may see blown up, it actually reconfigures the wiring of the brain, giving priority to those structures in the midbrain that have to do with fight or flight, the essentials that are protective mechanisms, and often cut off the contact with, or the processing of the higher order cerebral functions found in the cortex.

I will just give you one contemporary horrible situation: This sergeant who murdered 16 Afghan adults and children, as the story comes out; he allegedly had been drinking in the base. He had had multiple tours of duty in Iraq and Afghanistan, four tours in all. One cannot but wonder whether this is a similar pattern of the expression of PTSD, particularly to males returning from the field of combat to what one finds when they are provoked by something in an intimate partner relationship and then they turn on their spouses. In this scenario, there is a very disproportionate prevalence comparing, say, with returned servicemen with other people in the general population. We now have a substantial amount of research.

What is going on here between men and women? Why might we have these curious responses to one another as we come into this conference, mature, experienced, thoughtful, and sensitive people that we are? Are we beasts? Well, the answer is, to a certain extent, yes. Two neuroscientists at the University of Pennsylvania, and previously at Temple, are a husband and wife team named Rubin and Rachel Gerb. They were interested in understanding the social concomitants of blood flow in the frontal cortex. Blood flow can be measured very easily by attaching painless electrodes to the scalp. And their thought was to measure blood flow similar to the way you would look at a brainwave, using voltage differences. They measured the difference in blood flow between the frontal cortices of males and females in response to the social cues presented by their research assistants. And what they did in this study was to have the male and female adult volunteers sit in a chair as their male and female research assistants—Rubin and Rachel Gerb's assistants—approached them, making one or another facial or hand gestures.

Well, it was very striking, because there were really some important differences in the blood flow to the cortex, frontal cortex, of males and females. For one thing, where the female brains were continuously active, the blood flow was pretty much sustained across these different cues with greater or lesser degrees of modulation, male brains tended to turn on and off.

I just wanted to see who laughed at this, and it was more women than men who laughed. I mean, I think this may resonate in more than just in one way.

And what's more, it was a particular stimulus that really excited the blood flow of the male brain, and it was not the stimulus that some of you may think it was. It was rather another male's entering the field of vision, making a hostile threat. What's going on? Well, Rubin and Rachel Gerb published the findings of this research, very interesting, and they gave it a terrific interview to a science journalist named Rebecca Love, who published a marvelous book in 1998 called *Sex on the Brain*, provocative title, but full of very good material. They suggested that what was at issue here was a contemporary representation of an ancient survival mechanism, that for men to survive themselves and for them to protect their intimates, their families, the mothers of their children and the children themselves, they had to keep other men at bay. They had these well-developed alerting systems. And this might have to do indeed why in contemporary life very many men deal with the portent of threat, the entry by other men into their environments. Where, for women, the modulation of their blood flow and the continuous alertness to the social cues, they are determined by the survival mechanisms over generations and generations of evolutionary adaptation for females, which depended on relationships. They are nurturing. They are sustaining to protect them and the little people in evolutionary perspective who uniquely depended on them.

Furthermore, I was going to illustrate the Rubin and Rachel Gerb Study by using the clicker that was causing such a problem earlier. I don't need it and it isn't here now, anyway. I just wanted to have clicker in my hand because I was going to use it as a homey example of this in behavior with a television clicker. If a woman in this audience has recently had the pleasure of watching TV with a man, you know that for the most part he wants to hold the clicker in his hands. And, furthermore, where he may want first to see all of the offerings on all of the channels and possibly to surf between particular storylines which had to do with problem-solving, with action and threat and counter-threat and the like, you may quickly as a female become hooked on a story. And as the Gerbs suggest, the story may have to do importantly with relationships, with love, with romance, and other aspects of life experience. Anyway, I think you get the drift. We're different as males and females.

This May Lead to Controlling Behavior

Furthermore, as I interpret this life adaptation, this has to do with males' needs for controlling their environments. It is a life adaptation that under certain circumstances, with certain prefiguring childhood experiences in the background, can lead to distortions in controlling behavior.

Now, in no sense am I saying this to encourage sympathy for, and much less identification with, males' controlling behavior. But I feel that it is appropriate to offer a different set of conceptual tools with which to organize the data, apropos of which, having quoted a Supreme Court Judge, I want to also quote a distinguished psychologist, to pay tribute to the psychologists and the lawyers alike in the room. Abraham Maslow, the distinguished Brandeis professor unburdened himself with many aphorisms in the course of a wise and thoughtful career. And one of the ones that I like the most is his aphorism: If the only tool you have is a hammer, you tend to treat every problem as if it were a nail. And, as you know, one of the speakers suggested the need for a hammer to be used in regard to the family—broken family court system.

I think one has to be careful with that. A professor of statistics at Harvard School of Public Health with whom I worked very closely over the years restated the Maslow aphorism as follows. He said: if the only tool you have is a hammer, you tend to treat every problem as if it were a thumb. So you have to be very careful in your use of this.

Okay. So what I want to do is quickly to turn to the matter at hand and actually to return to the previous speaker's very apt quotation of the work of Neil Jacobson and John Gottman, who wrote the book *When Men Batter Women* in 1998. In that interview, Jacobson said, apropos of the distinction that you heard before about pit bulls and cobras, and I just want you to hear this in Jacobson's own words, "Pit bulls are great guys until they get to intimate relationships." O.J. Simpson is a classic pit bull. In that interview, they stated that pit bulls confine their monstrous behavior to the women they love, acting out of emotional dependence and a fear of abandonment. Pit bulls are loved by everyone except their wives and girlfriends. Toward them they are the stalkers, the jealous husbands, and boyfriends.

And just a couple of other comments: Pit bulls are, he added, quick to see betrayal, and it infuriates them so that (these are not his words but mine) their fury explodes into violence because they appear to lose control as their violence grows out of a dependency they feel has been betrayed. Pit bulls often portray themselves as the ones who have been victimized in the violent relationship. And you may recall that O.J. Simpson wrote a book in which he claims that he was the victim; he was the battered husband. The victim wasn't Nicole Brown Simpson whom he was alleged to have murdered.

Where cobras are relatively free of webs of emotional dependence and their intended spheres of influence are not compartmentalized like the pit bulls. They have a powerful need to be the boss and to make sure that everyone, and particularly their wives and girlfriends, submit. They are not motivated by jealousy, love, and dependence, but by unsentimental antisocial attitudes. They are more likely to be aggressive towards strangers and pets as well as friends, relatives, and cobras than are the pit bulls. When they think their dominance has been challenged, cobras strike swiftly and ferociously. In a coldblooded way, cobras may use violence to establish complete control in a relationship and then back off and maintain the dominance with verbal threats.

Now, just briefly to return to the brain and our wiring as human beings: There is another aspect of cobras that students of males who batter are familiar with, although I entirely agree that the knowledge base is far from sufficient. It is that when the cobras are at their worst and most dangerous, when they are being violent towards intimates, their pulse rates go down. They are the so-called vagal batterers. It is the vagus nerves.

So I see they are giving me 10 minutes, but I would respectfully like to ask for 10 minutes more, given the fact that one of the speakers did not come and because you all are so generous and because I started with something out of my field that I know you will find helpful. I am going to be talking about some fairly serious things, but I promise you at the very end I am going to tell the first real joke of the day that has to do with a controlling man and a woman with a wonderful saucy perspective on dealing with their relationship. But that is to follow. That is a promissory note.

Pit bulls get very physiologically aroused as their fury rises, but cobras calm down internally as they become more physically or verbally assaultive. Their pulses go down rather than up. And this vagus nerve mediated response has led some students of battering men to characterize them as vagal abusers. The vagus nerve deals with the control of the physiological systems such as heart rate, vascular dilatation, and it is, if you will, a paradoxical effect, but it is very, very important to realize that we are dealing with physiological issues, not just psychological quirks. And I did not mean that in any way by suggesting psychological quirks as any kind of an aspersion on psychologists and their instrumentation.

When the police are called to intervene in a marital situation provoked by a cobra, they often find a hysterical woman and a very calm man who explains that it was all the woman's doing. Sometimes the police accept the cobra's story and arrest the wrong person, the woman who has been assaulted.

Now, I want to just make a parenthetical comment about PTSD, extending the important point that Toby made. For those of us who are involved frequently in the court processing of the children's custody, we know how deeply the women feel about their children's suffering, the depth of worry, the generalized sense of anxiety about the children.

My wife, Carolyn, here toward the front was the principal investigator of a very important study, actually the first federally funded study beginning in 1985, of the responses to children's disclosures of sexual abuse by their mothers. And over the course of the year, very careful study with three different data points using standardized measures of anxiety and depression, Carolyn demonstrated one of the key underpinnings of PTSD in the mothers, that the mothers in the course of the year had pronounced elevations into the clinical range of measures of anxiety, which for some women sustained well beyond the initial period. So in most women, their anxiety rises when they have been protective of their children, but women who have previously been sexually victimized often had sustained elevations of their levels of anxiety, suggesting that this was, if you will, a retraumatization of these women.

My point here is, however, to present an alternative formulation for what we see in court circumstances that sometimes are profoundly misinterpreted by judges. It has to do with women being traumatized by both their children's victimization and the process that accuses them of making it all up, thus giving undue credence to the exculpatory comments by the lawyers for the perpetrator and the perpetrator in testimony himself. This is a horrible experience and a traumatizing experience, I and others believe, and may account for some of the hyper-arousability of women in these settings that can be misinterpreted by the judge as defiance of their authorities. Because of this lack of understanding, the punitive dynamics get established in these cases, especially in those corrupt court systems. This is where the judge appoints evaluators and, for example, a guardian *ad litem*, who are political cronies. And I think that all of us who work in this area know well the feeling of walking into these courtrooms where there is all of this knowledgeable chatter among people who work with one another and often the judges are there like queen bees. And, indeed, some of the female judges really see this as a miniature country club for them, as people come in with discordant attitudes and raise uncomfortable issues as well, whereby the women are marginalized, and they are subsequently punished, if you will.

So, anyway, I think that women are wired more than men to internalize concern for children, and what's more, as Lenore pointed out this morning so beautifully, women's relationships are more textured, personal, intimate, and complex than men's. As well, there are data, very good data, that from early childhood women are permitted to feel and to express a much broader pallet of emotions than are boys and men. And this goes to the expressivity that we see in women as opposed to, say, the control that we see in cobras on the witness stand.

The Bareness of Men's Lives

Now, it is actually as has been pointed out, that the studies of these men are really insufficient, but the real insights, I think, come from the arts. And I just want to give you one by a wonderful poet, Anais Nin, who was also a playwright. I think she is probably best known for her erotica, but she was a very serious student of relationships. In her play, *The Four-Chambered Heart*, the female protagonist and users lie to men who live on shoals, "how heavy this life, this life of men. Is it true they cannot raise one eyebrow without the other? So weighted with their work eagerly curving their shoulders to the contours of the yoke? A world dry to tears and bleached of color. One never hears the wind chimes or the music of jewelry. In the mornings they brush away their dreams like flies. There is no carpet and no grass over the rough, brown boards of their existence. Perhaps, never owning more than two pairs of shoes, the richness of life has escaped them." It is really beautiful, but tremendously telling about the barrenness of men's lives.

Men Doing Unbelievable Things

And while I am at it, before descending into the unbelievable things that men do and giving some glossing with the conceptual framework that I tried to provide, I also wanted to talk about another very important issue for boys and men, and that has to do with trust in relationships.

When one works with men, one of the things that one has got to do—and I was just talking to the judge who works for the National Council on Juvenile and Family Courts Judges about this—because I certainly try to do this in my practice and I know that you did as a lawyer and then as a judge—is that you have to establish some line of communication with them based on some sliver of experience or attribute that you can respect or even like so you can communicate with them, give them a sense that you are a person who will listen to them, notwithstanding some of the horrible things that they have done. And in order to do this, it requires a little bit of effort in many situations, but it is vital to do. And then very frequently as a physician or as a psychologist, certainly as a judge, you are able to use your authority to enable them to see reality, to deport themselves in a more responsible way. It requires some effort, but it can be done. And it goes to forming and sustaining trust.

Erik Erikson made a brilliant comment. He is the psychologist who was psychoanalytically-oriented, but who proposed really an alternative to the traditional psychoanalytical theory that dealt with dualisms that will lead to reconcile between early infancy and old age. Erikson characterized the primary dualism in infancy, over which everything else is constructed, is trust versus basic mistrust. And apropos of this, he made these brief comments in one of his writings on children who are deprived of basic mistrust. "We cannot know what happens in a baby, but direct observation as well as overwhelming clinical experience indicate that early mistrust is accompanied by an experience of 'total rage,' with fantasies of the total domination or even destruction of the sources of pleasure and provision, and that such fantasies and rages live on in the individual and are revived in extreme cases and situations."

What he is talking about here is what I think many of us would refer to as men's dependency needs, and I actually agree that the pit bull-cobra formulation is not sufficiently nuanced around issues of men's dependency. I think that this is one of the reasons why for many of these guys you don't know what's going to happen next.

Anyway, briefly, I just want to talk about one set of clinical examples of men doing unbelievable things. In my clinic at Children's Hospital, I remember one of the debriefing sessions that we did all the time. This one was with the father and his lawyer. This is a man who admitted that he had physically abused his wife and children, even recommended by the judge as a condition of continued visitation of any kind with his children to enter a domestic violence intervention program. In Massachusetts, we have certified programs that are quite sound. The man tentatively agreed to do this as I was talking with him, but his lawyer, who mirrored many of his worst characterological aspects, argued with him in front of me: "But, wait a minute. Your wife caused this whole thing. What are you doing agreeing to go into this?" And I had to struggle in that interview with his lawyer who ostensibly was objecting on his client's behalf.

In another situation, the father who anally penetrated and spanked both young sons with an identified plastic implement, the bruises from which conforms with its outlines on photographs that I interpreted, was given full custody of both children. The mother, a child psychologist, was referred for treatment to rid her of her belief that her sons were abused. When she reported those treating her to the licensing board, as these were licensed psychologists in the state of North Carolina, the board started action against them.

At this point, they recommended that her visitations be stopped, and the court accepted this. It was only after there was subsequent severe medical neglect, along with allegations that the judge had colluded with the father's counsel in an inappropriate way (i.e., the judge's husband worked for the law firm that did business with the father's counsel), did the judge recuse herself and the mother's visitation contact resume.

In another current case, in which I am involved, the mother had concerns about her husband's obsessive massaging of her son's thighs and genitals that was evidenced to observing adults in public settings. Her concern to seek medical care for her child's penile pain and infection and chronic anal fissures was derided. She was characterized by a psychiatric proponent of parental alienation syndrome who actually was chosen by the chief judge in the family court to evaluate the case, and this guy called her a perpetrator of Munchausen Syndrome by Proxy for seeking evaluations of her child. The judge characterized the mother's behavior as a woman who would do anything to prove that her son had been sexually abused. The kid had disclosed to a therapist. He had very many physical examination concomitants including these anal fissures, and the judge, friends with the GAL, who then immediately subsequent to the case was proposed by the governor of the state to become a family court judge herself, decided to go entirely with GAL's recommendation, totally dismissing any of the serious and careful and totally well-trained professionals who had given testimony in this case.

In another situation, there were two cases in which I had been involved as a consultant. In this last example, but which gives the hinge for the interpretation of these actions, in two different cases, skin lesions were produced in the course of weekend visitations by the fathers of children, which then lasted through the subsequent week. In one case, the child's skin was abraded by scraping the skin and then into those abrasions was rubbed fecal matter, feces, from the toilet, according to the child's disclosures, and the infections of the skin that I saw photographs of clearly demonstrated this. In another contemporary case, the man used household cleanser to scrape into the skin and to produce a repeated contact dermatitis.

What was going on here? This, in my opinion, was a metaphorical example—a metaphorical domestic violence. The intent was not just to harm and intimidate the child as in one of these cases this man also used these hurtful actions to subordinate a child prior to sexually abusing the child. But in both cases, it is my belief that the lingering skin signs on the children would be a continuing marker about the man's control.

I see all of these situations as artifacts of controlling behavior by the men that took the form of assault that took the form of lasting injury.

Anyway, on that sad note, I just want to lighten the tone with a quick story that will lead to your forgiving me for taking this extra bit of time. So this is a family representation in a story. It is the family of American nostalgia, in which a woman greets her husband at the end of the day. He comes home from work, and she is in the house, keeping house, and at the door she says, "Honey, the dishwasher is broken. It is making a racket. There are suds on the floor. I really have no idea what's going on." And he says, "Who do you think I am, the Maytag man? Just pick up the phone and call and the guy will come and fix it." The following day the guy comes home and the wife meets him at the door and says, "The vacuum cleaner is broken. I don't know what's going on here. There's dust in the air. I can't get the carpets clean. It's all this noise." And the guy says, "Who do you think I am, the Hoover man? You know, just bring it in and it will get taken care of." The next night the guy comes home from work. His wife meets him at the door and says, "Honey, do you know Henry next door?" The guy says, "Yeah." She says, "Well, he was over this afternoon.

And guess what. The dishwasher is fixed and the vacuum cleaner is fixed." So the guy thinks for a second, and he said, "Well, what did you have to do to get him to do all that?" And she says, "Well, he gave me a choice: either I could have sex with him or I could bake him a cake." So the guy thinks again and he says, "Well, what kind of cake did you bake him?" And she says, "Who do you think I am, Betty Crocker?"

Thank you for your indulgence.

Chapter 13
Estrangement and NOT Parental Alienation Disorder

Leslie Drozd, Ph.D.

DR. JANET CUMMINGS: Our next speaker is Dr. Leslie Drozd, who is a psychologist, author, family court judge, and family court system educator and trainer, and she helped create the New Model Standards for Conducting Child Custody Evaluations for the Association of Family Conciliation Courts. She will be speaking to us on the subject that has been mentioned in a number of the talks: estrangement and parental alienation syndrome. Dr. Drozd.

DR. DROZD: Good afternoon, everyone. I am glad to be here. Thanks.

So it is not parental alienation syndrome I am talking about. It is estrangement, not parental alienation disorder. The difference is as you will see in a minute.

So I am going to try something first here real quickly. An individual has been described by a neighbor as follows: Steve is very shy and withdrawn, invariably helpful, but with little interest in people or in the world of reality. A neat and tidy soul, he has a need for order and structure and a passion for detail. Is Steve more likely to be a librarian or a farmer?

Librarian?

Farmer?

Because the description of Steve is aligned with what we would stereotypically think of someone being like that would be a librarian, but if you look at that statistically, there are a whole lot more male farmers than there are male librarians. My point of this is: Sometimes we have first impressions of people. We have first impressions by stereotypical descriptions. Such as, the wife is hysterical, the mother is hysterical, and from the start you begin to form assumptions.

So, consider three different things: parental alienation syndrome, alienating behavior, and parental alienation disorder. Gardner was the first to propose the concept of parental alienation syndrome, and he defined it as a child's unjustified campaign of denigration against a parent that results from a combination of two contributing factors: one being programming or brainwashing by a parent, and the other one, the child's own contributions to the vilification of the targeted parent.

Parental Alienation: Syndrome or Disorder?

In 2001, this started to be known by another term; that is: parental alienation or alienating behavior and that was something that Johnston and Kelly, et al., in Northern California came up with. It was still fairly similar, but more of an emphasis on the child's behavior and the child's symptoms. And more recently, unfortunately—talk about recycling things—we are now facing recycling of PAS to now PAB, which is now called a behavior disorder. The thing we are recycling it to is parental alienation disorder, which I will get to in a second. So a decade ago, we had Kelly and Johnston expand the thinking so that people started to think of parental alienation as something that had to do with children's behavior. They define an alienated child as one who expresses freely and persistently unreasonable negative feelings and beliefs, such as anger, hatred, rejection, or fear, towards a parent that is disproportional to the child's actual experience with that parent.

They further define children who have reasonable cause to have such attitudes and belief as those who are estranged. So that was not the main emphasis of what they wrote about in 2001, as "estranged" was only one part in that publication. In fact, when I first read the Johnston and Kelly work, I actually did not even see "estranged," and so a colleague of mine, Nancy Oleson, and I started to look at other reasons why this might happen.

So in 2004 and again in 2010, Dr. Oleson and I expanded the Kelly and Johnston theory, and before we turn to that, let me go back to this new thing, Parental Alienation Disorder (PAD). It is really a recycling of Parental Alienation Syndrome (PAS) in my opinion. PAD as it has been proposed to be in the next "Diagnostic and Statistics Manual," does not make a distinction between when a child has this disorder and estrangement. There are now diagnostic criteria for this proposed disorder, but I and several others in the room are vehemently opposed to this diagnosis being put in the DSM.

There are three main reasons for this opposition. First, there are insufficient empirical data to support the benefits of adding this. Secondly, the reason for adding this is probably one of reimbursement insurance ion a situation where there are insufficient data to differentiate symptoms from trauma, specifically child abuse and domestic violence from this disorder. Finally, if there is a realistic reason for the child not to want to spend time with a parent, they would still be labeled with PAD should this be one of the diagnoses. As Walker and Shapiro pointed out in 2010 in the *Journal of Child Custody*, there is insufficient data to demonstrate the necessity of the court using PAD to force reunification of children with an alienated parent in order for them to grow up healthy.

The Oleson and Drozd Alternative

And so going back to Dr. Oleson and me, by extending we thought that the first thing you needed to do was look at the safety of the child and then if a child is rejecting a parent or resisting contact, there might be three different main reasons, one of them being, it's normal. Perhaps you have got a teenager identifying with a parent of the same gender. It also could be poor parenting, in which there are several kinds of poor parenting, one of that being alienating behavior; and the third is, it could be some sort of abuse.

We actually looked at that again in 2010, and when we looked at it in 2010, we clarified that a little bit more. And this is the 2010 version of it. Normal development, the same as it was before, but there could be different kinds of abuse that could be causing the child not wanting to spend time with a parent. One is child abuse. Another is substance abuse. Another was intimate partner violence. And certainly there could be parenting problems that could cause a child not to want to spend time. If I had my preference and could rewrite the English language, which I am not so grandiose to think that I can do, the word "alienation" would never be used in a case where there is any abuse. You might call it sabotaging. You could call it other terms. Nancy Oleson and I have tried that for 10 years, and I would tell you we have not been very successful. Some people are using the word "sabotaging" now, but I do not know that people have stopped using the word "alienation."

Another term that people are starting to use, so I want to make you aware of that, is people are starting to talk about gate keeping. There being three different kinds of gate keeping: there is facilitative gate keeping, which is facilitating the relationship with the other parent. In my view that depends upon whether the other parent is such that you would want to facilitate the relationship. Would that really be in the child's best interests?

On the other end of the continuum is restrictive gatekeeping where a parent is on purpose restricting access. There could be many reasons, which actually are the reasons.

Those two have been talked about in the literature. The third one that I have added is protective gate keeping in which there could be a genuine cause for the parent not to want the child to be with the other parent. I have called that protected gatekeeping. We are just writing about all of these things right now, so it can be hard to give you a reference for it other than conferences many of us have spoken at.

So there are many different hypotheses and I am going to go through each one of these.

Affinity is a close relationship with a parent that might lead to a little bit of distance from a child in the midst of a divorce where the parents are not getting along might—commonsense another parent. There is nothing pathological about that.

Alignment might have them align with one parent more than the other, just because they have got to get themselves out of the middle. I think that is good adaptation on their part, and to do that, they may align with one parent more than the other. Still, I am not sure that is pathological. You start to get further right on the decision tree, I think you potentially have got some pathology going on. Certainly you all know what child abuse is, substance abuse minima, partner violence. The part I want to point out here is that a child can have two different kinds of reactions to abuse, any one of those kinds, the intimate partner violence being what has been talked about most today.

The child could *identify with the aggressor*. That is not written about much, but we do see it a lot. You especially see that with a teenage child who is a male teenage child, assuming that the aggressive parent (the abuser) is the father, and you see that child identifying with the father. You have already got to poll developmentally for that to happen. Consider that the child sits there and thinks, now who's got the money, who has got all the power, and who has got all of the control, who can give me what I want. I do not want to look like my mom because she looks kind of poor and pathetic. And if I just stay close to this guy, my dad, and then he won't do to me what he did to my mom. That is identification with the aggressor. It is a term taken from psychoanalytic literature, but I think it fits with this group.

There is *estrangement*, the child is scared. It is what we have been talking about, some sort of post-traumatic stress disorder, some sort of reason, a realistic reason. So if you go back in your mind to the decision tree that Johnston and Kelly had in 2001, what Drozd and Oleson have done now is emphasize the estrangement as a possibility. So that can occur with any one of the kinds of abuse that we have up there.

And I certainly think the parents' behavior, either the parent who has been abused or the other parent, could engage in some sort of *sabotaging of the other parent*. I would rather use that word if there is abuse, for whatever power I have to change the English language. I think that when you have children not wanting to spend time with a parent, one of many reasons could be one of the parents could be sabotaging. Or if there is no abuse, I would call it *alienating* the child from the other parent. That does exist. I understand with this audience that may get me stoned up here, but the reality is that happens. Okay? I just think it gets all mucked up with the abuse. And I think people forget the estrangement.

The child—the parent could not be attuned with the child. One parent can be *intrusive*. There is a great book in which Barbara Oleson was the main author on intrusive parenting, the kind of parenting where a parent takes over the child, and that happens in a lot of these cases we have been talking about today, is intrusive parenting. A parent can be too lax or too rigid in terms of discipline, that a parent could be self-centered. The word "narcissism" was used. How in the world could you be a good parent if you are battering the other parent? You are certainly being self-centered. And one that has been talked about more recently—and I have seen a lot—is *enmeshment*, where one parent is enmeshed; that is, there are no boundaries between that parent and that child. If one were to sum up my career since 2000, I could do it in one word, and that is "and," a-n-d. I think this field looks at things as it is this or it is this, and my sense is it is "and." Now, which one of those things you want to pick up—there you get quite a smorgasbord you could pick for any given case. I think it is rarely one thing or the other.

Protective and Restrictive Gatekeeping

As I mentioned before, there can be protective and restrictive gatekeeping. I think protective gatekeeping is something that occurs when there is estrangement, when there is poor parenting, when there has been exposure to domestic violence, and, in particular, child sexual abuse. Restricted gatekeeping, other terms, or synonyms that might be used for that would be alienation if there are false allegations of any kind of abuse, enmeshment, or some sort of sabotaging behavior.

You can have hybrid cases. You can have every possible combination. You could have alienation and estrangement. You could have alienation and enmeshment; estrangement and enmeshment; alienation-estrangement—you get the idea. You could have "and." You could have many different combinations.

Who is most likely to be the parent who is engaging in alienating behavior, if you want to call it that. I am calling it sabotaging behavior. In a preliminary study done in 2005 by Jan Johnston, et al., the results are not surprising. It is what I see clinically. The person who is more likely to engage in the alienating or sabotaging behavior is the abusive parent. Think about it logically. They are the ones with more power, more control. This includes the money. They are the ones that are more likely to use it as a means to get back at the victim parent. They are more likely to be the one engaging in sabotaging behavior, which some would call alienating behavior.

If you will quickly look at the very recent research, there is a new book that is out by the Oxford University Press in January of this year. Titled *Parenting Plan Evaluations: Applied Research for Family Court,*" in that book Dr. Kingley and I have gathered together the most recent research in all sorts of areas having to do with family law and parenting plan evaluations. There is a chapter in there by Jennifer Hardesty, et al., including Michael Johnson, on domestic violence. There is a chapter in there by Mike Siney, Jan Johnston, Barbara Fidler, and Nick Bala on alienation. There are a jillion other chapters as well.

Different Kinds of Abuse

So I pulled a few things from that about alienation, which ought to make all of you quite apprehensive about somebody throwing this term around. There remains no consensus of a single definition for alienation. The evidence that supports alienation is largely based upon clinical opinions and expert opinions and not solid research. Further research is needed to distinguish alienation from other types of strained parent-child relationships. And a standard rating system is needed to assess the strengths and limitations of current empirical research specific to alienation.

Siney, Johnston, Fidler, and Bala came up with a way to rate different studies, and, bless Jan Johnston's heart, her studies were rated medium-to-low in terms of reliability and validity, but you cannot get much better than that with the initial place all of that is in the field. So I will tell you, I was careful if I used that term in court before, but now I'm really careful after having read Chapter 13 in that book.

There are many different kinds of abuse that people can have, and I think that we tend to get them all mixed up. There are levels of physical aggression and there are levels of psychological aggression, and each may be high, medium, or low. There can be high psychological aggression and low physical aggression. Now, I would say that probably means one of the parents is engaging in pretty much a course of control, high emotional abuse, psychological abuse, but maybe there have been one or two incidents of physical abuse. That's domestic violence. And the children are affected by that. Or you can have obviously medium, you can have medium of both psychological and physical aggression. You can have medium of the psychological aggression and high physical aggression. Usually we don't miss that. Anytime you get on the high score on physical aggression, people do not tend to miss it.

The one that would be missed: low on psychological aggression, high on physical aggression. I do not see that much, and the reason is, if you have got high on physical aggression, usually the psychological aggression is there as well. And there is the one in which you have high on both.

So let's take a look at intimate partner violence. Dr. Shapiro has looked through the literature and looked at risk assessment, so this is basically a summary of a lot of the views he had to say. This is a way to describe domestic violence or intimate partner violence in a relationship, and I think that we make mistakes by not looking at all of these different factors.

The first one you ought to look at is *risk*. The things in the research that tend to be very highly correlated with high risk are history of previous violence. Dr. Shapiro spoke about that: substance abuse, major mental disorders, which would include major depression, bipolar disorder, and some psychotic disorders, and then certainly you need to look at a threat assessment in terms of, has someone made a threat? Has there been obsessive following, that is, stalking, are there any weapons? A judge in Los Angeles who used to be a sheriff's officer asked one question in a hearing for a temporary restraining order: "Sir, do you have any weapons?" He says yes or no. "Ma'am, does he have any weapons?" If there are any weapons, either one of them has said weapons, he issues the temporary. Obviously that does not mean for sure it happened because there has not been a hearing, but the temporary he at least issues, then. What's the kind of aggression? Is it physical, emotional, or psychological—And/or is there coercive control that is involved, which can be a combination of those things. Is there a pattern? What is the frequency? What is the severity? Have the children been exposed? And what is the pattern of instigation? Is it primarily the male partner, the female partner, mutual, or defensive or reactive?

People at this point in the field are talking about categories of different kinds of domestic violence. Part of what my co-authors and I are thinking is that the categories do not hold up to the research. You can't make a distinction between people based upon the categories, but you can upon continuous variables. Although some of the variables can be reflected by yes or no, a large number of them occur along a continuum. They are continuous variables, and that is what ought to be reported. The major ones being talked about are course of control—we have changed the name a little bit—or conflict instigators are situations specific or separation associated. With regard to conflict instigators, situation specific, or separation associated, you may only be seeing the tip of the iceberg. So it is important to do a thorough assessment to see if other elements are there, because that is going to make a difference in terms of parenting.

What do we do at the family court that gravitates towards simple solutions to complex problems? I am not blaming the family court alone. I think all of us do that.

[At this point Dr. Drozd showed a video of a basketball game with the instruction to count how many times the players wearing white pass the basketball. The correct number of passes is 15 and most viewers got that right, but did they see the gorilla in the background?]

Male voice on video: "Count how many times the players wearing white pass the basketball."

DR. DROZD: Count. Okay? Watch carefully.

[Video shown.]

Male voice on video: "How many passes did you count? The correct answer is 15 passes. But did you see the gorilla?"

[Video rewound and shown.]

Male voice: "This video is from research by Daniel Simons and Christopher Chabris and is copyrighted. It is available for use in talks, training, and teaching on DVDs from Viscog Productions. Learn more at theinvisiblegorilla.com.

DR. DROZD: So how many—honestly, how many of you saw the gorilla? Okay. A good number of you. Pardon me? But you had already stopped counting.

Most people—I mean, I had a room full of AAML attorneys and more than a smattering of judges, and most people did not see the gorilla. And what does that speak to? Why is that relevant? It is relevant because all of us in the different roles, we miss things. We miss big things. We miss the gorilla in the middle of the room. We miss things that are right in front of us.

System 1 and 2 Thinking

There is a wonderful book in which the research basically reveals what we are saying. The research shows that we should not trust our gut. Now, that is really controversial amongst mental health professionals. That is what we think we are trained to do, and it's wrong, especially with this issue.

Daniel Kahneman in 2011 wrote an outstanding book. If you have not read it, it is well worth your while. It is called *Thinking Fast and Slow*, and although he does not talk about custody evaluations I am translating it into custody evaluations. Basically, he says that we have two kinds of thinking: System 1, which is automatic. It is the first hit. It is the intuitive reaction. We all need that. You're driving on the freeway and all of a sudden you move over two lanes. You don't know why you moved over two lanes. And then you find out that there was an accident behind you because there was a drunk driver to your left. Thank goodness you had that reaction. But it is not the best thing to be doing in cases that are as complex as this. System 2 thinking: We, all of us, overestimate our accuracy in System 1. In fact, what people do if they stick with System 1 is that the fervor that they have behind that assumption is strong, and if you cannot challenge it with more rational, logical thinking, which is System 2 thinking, then they have made an error in thinking. This is one of the major problems that people do that was being talked about earlier, that Dr. Benjamin was talking about in custody evaluations. It is part of what any of us doing trainings are trying to offset.

The thing is that System 1 thinking is easy. It does not lower our blood sugar levels. It does not make us work any harder. It just comes to us. And System 2 thinking is conscious. You have to go through something like the decision trees that I have put up there. You need to look at hypotheses and test them back and forth, like Dr. Benjamin was talking about, and that all takes time and it takes energy. So think about the judge's situation. There was actually a study done in Israel about the judge and the kinds of decisions made in the morning when his blood sugar levels are higher and then think about the decisions made in the afternoon when blood sugar levels are lower. Perhaps one of the interventions is we ought to provide apples for judges on the bench, not M&Ms, because we will go "whoop," up and down too quick, but later in the day. In the study done in Israel, what was found was that the decisions that were made in the afternoon were off the cuff: slight fine; slam the book at them; no, let him off. The decisions were more nuanced and thought through in the morning.

So when intuition and heuristics are not enough, forensic and legal rules require that you articulate the basis of your opinion and recommendations and forensic and legal rules require that another person could examine your data and reach an independent conclusion. The System 1 thinking does not work for that. You might use System 1 to figure out if you are safe enough in your office in terms of threat assessment for yourself, but that is not how to think through these complex things. It is resorted to for lots of reasons, such as lack of resources, time problems, all sorts of problems, of why that is resorted to. System 1 thinking is also resorted to because it is easier, and I think some of us in the field have gotten a bit lazy.

For example, people are more likely to choose unhealthy temptation foods like chocolate cake when they have done mentally demanding tasks, as in System 2.

On the other hand, people are more likely to choose healthy foods like fruit salad when they have done easy, undemanding tasks like System 1. Given the potential failure rates of intuition and heuristics, you need to design a process that moves against the common tendency to error and potential failure. You can see I have spoken about potential failure rates of intuition and heuristics. You must use slower, more effortful, logical processes, and one example might be in using some sort of decision tree.

Thanks, everybody.

Chapter 14
Second Panel Discussion

DR. JANET CUMMINGS: The panel is assembled, and are there any questions?

FIRST AUDIENCE SPEAKER: Yes, thank you. First of all, I just wanted to ask Dr. Leslie Drozd a question, and maybe even Dr. David Shapiro. With regards to the issue of risk factors, my review of some of the research that I have done with regards to risk assessment and also predictability of clinical risk assessment to violence, I thought one thing maybe to consider: first would be a history of whether or not there was victimization, early victimization, of the alleged perpetrator; for example, either by domestic violence, sexual abuse, physical violence, or some other form of victimization.

And then also I did not see a reference to traumatic brain injury, which I understand is a huge contributor for lack of internal control mechanisms, which often, quite frankly, impact juveniles, particularly those with great disparities in terms of resource.

DR. DROZD: Let me comment real briefly. I think we have included under "history of previous violence" it going both ways. When I have spoken about this for a longer period of time than a few minutes, I have talked about those. I think you are actually right. The traumatic brain injury is not on there and should be.

JUDGE LERNER-WREN: And then just lastly, in terms of entire contexts of conversations, something else I really did not hear, even though in this particular presentation per se I think it has a lot of relevance. It has to do with the cultural competency and contact, the texture, in terms of who we are talking about. I was just reading about it for this week's class that I was preparing before I came here hurriedly. It's fabulous, and maybe we will talk about it later. It is one of Professor Michael Perlin's pieces actually having to do with the United Nations Convention for the Rights of Disabled. It deals with the importance of really being highly sensitive to and trained in the area of evaluation where it comes to cultural competency as to not only the culture of the nation of origin but also how these simulations have gone, if you will, in terms of the simulation to the host country.

So I just wanted to add a little bit of texture to that because I know it is important.

DR. SHAPIRO: Let me just respond to a few of the points that Judge Wren made.

Number one, you are absolutely right. These risk assessment instruments are very poor in terms of any of the multicultural dimensions. They really need to be refined a great deal along those lines.

The second point, where you asked about the victimization, that is part of the SARA. Now, being either the victim of or a witness to family violence, that is one of the dimensions there.

And the third point you—oh, the brain trauma. Yeah. The brain trauma was in the original McArthur studies. That was one of the five—you know, it was sociological, psychological, biological/neurological variables. They did look at it. That has not carried over from the more generalized violence. We know definitely it is involved in the generalized violence, but it has not carried over into the domestic violence literature at all.

DR. WALKER: I would agree with what everybody is saying. I want to add, though—because I think it is really important for us to remember—that we are talking about batterers as if the only part of their behavior we are concerned about is their violence. Many of these men that I have worked with or that I have studied also have severe mental illnesses. They are bipolar. They are paranoid, or they have delusional disorders, and some of those mental illnesses have higher risks of violent behavior than others. And so if we only put them in anger management classes or in domestic violence classes, it is simply not enough. Learning to readjust your attitudes towards women and towards society is certainly important, but it is not going to stop the violence. Learning how to stop your drinking or your other addictive behavior is very important, but it is not enough to stop your violence. And so these are—these combinations of things that Dr. Drozd was talking about are really important for us. We tend to get narrower and narrower and narrower in our thinking about whom we are dealing with, and for my wonderful legal colleagues who think that their role of psychologists in custody is superfluous, I suggest that, for some of these men who have these mental disorders, you will not see it and you will need us and you may not even know that you will need us. So even though I do not think we are doing a great job, I do not want to throw us out quite yet. I am not quite ready.

SECOND AUDIENCE SPEAKER: Okay, thank you. Well, my problem is that I agree with people that have said opposite things. Oh, yeah, right. Okay. So I am trying to reconcile what people have said. A couple of people have said there's too much mental health evaluation that is cluttering up, it is unnecessary, it is a financial drain on the system, etc. And yet a more recent speaker presented a model evaluation system that I find quite interesting, so I want to propose something and see how people respond.

One thing I really appreciate about your evaluation system, Dr. Benjamin, is that you developed it over time. It was very systematic and progressive in its development, so you worked out all the kinks and you have got a pretty good model. Of course the downside of that, maybe you will sell it for $100 a person to people who do not have the money, but somewhere—it costs a lot of money if you are doing a very thorough job.

You also mentioned that you are getting a high rate of settlement, which in this room normally would scare us, because normally when settlements are typically made, my understanding is that they are typically made because the lawyers tell their clients: This is what the judge is going to decide so if we can agree on that now, you save a lot of money on the trial. So, normally, we are afraid of settlements that come out of, say, mediation between unequal parties. On the other hand, if you are doing such a good evaluation in identifying the abuse and identifying the domestic violence, then a settlement coming out of that, I'm guessing, might actually be a more equitable settlement that not only people can live with, but that actually it protects children and that would save not only litigation then but later. There are some real discrepancies and I would like to hear comments about that.

DR. BENJAMIN: First of all, I wish I had the empirical evidence to show that the outcomes from settlements have all been, you know, less child abuse, you know, less major modifications, less violence, and all the rest of it. I have not done that study, and, unfortunately, I do not know anybody who has done those studies, and we need to do those studies. And I am as culpable as everybody else in this room for not doing those studies.

I might, from my point of view, if we can lay out very systematic recommendations to protect the health of the children, and the settlements result from the evidence that the lawyers incorporate in their discussions and negotiations with each other and both parties have relatively good lawyers—that's a big "if," right?—then we are way ahead. We are way ahead for that family, because, in large part, you know, you are going to get the kids protected and it is going to be tens of thousands of dollars less spent, given the legal litigation process.

THIRD AUDIENCE SPEAKER: I just want to make something clear from my position as a woman. It is that one of the biggest problems is the failure within the court system as it exists to have the qualifications of the people who are doing evaluations scrupulously adhered to. And also that there needs to be less fear, if you will, of having actual evidence, where people are testifying and being cross-examined, both as to their credentials and as to their fact-findings. Cross-examination is known—we use this in the law—we say all the time it's the search for the truth. The ability to cross-examine someone on what they believe what they are saying is true or how they got to that belief or giving them hypotheticals to undermine it really is the basis of why we have this adversarial system at all, and it is the basis of how it works.

But we have circumstances where an order gets entered based on a report. I'm not talking settlement here; that's a whole different issue. I am talking about an order based on a report and an order gets entered and it has never had the chance to be questioned or undermined. It takes on a life of its own, and especially where we know we are using non-credentialed people, we have here a desperate circumstance for protecting.

DR. WALKER: I think psychologists have to take some responsibility. We have trained our colleagues as generalists, and in our ethics code we claim that psychologists are supposed to police themselves and only practice in areas in which they are qualified. I suggest that it may be high time for psychologists to start looking at specialization rather than only generalist training. We have so much knowledge today, and I do not believe any one of us has all the knowledge in all fields. And I do not think it is the lawyers' and judges' jobs to know who is a specialist in a particular area. It is our job and we should be able to give that information and put it out.

Now, there will be some people who are very smart and who will pass a test and say they are specialized and they are not. And we will have to work with that kind of lack of competency. But it certainly would make a big difference. APA and my own faculty fight over it, and we are pretty split in terms of whether we should or we shouldn't do the specialization, and I think that, Dr. John Caccavale, you were absolutely right: it comes right down to dollars and cents and who is going to make a living and who isn't.

DR. CACCAVALE: Today has really been good. It was a good day because I think we have had a really great discussion. But truth in fact is that I am going away from here with the same ideas that I had; that is, I do not think that we are being honest. I know that we can be good clinicians and I know that we can give good clinical decisions. My problem is that it goes to what Dr. Lenore Walker was saying: We are trying to offer decisions based upon things that we know very little about. That is the first step. If we listen to Dr. David Shapiro, if we listen to everyone else that has talked, our psychological tests are not tests. They are not at all that. We try to interpret, you know, testing; that is absolutely ridiculous. I have been involved in cases where evaluators have gone in using the House-Tree-Person test and the Rorschach test to justify their recommendations. This is absolutely outrageous. One of the points that I tried to make before was that psychologists tend to believe in different systems of human behavior. We are not unified with it. So consequently you have people who are psychoanalytically-oriented; other people that are more cognitively-oriented, behavior-oriented. This is something that is important: How we see the world. We do not go into court and openly state, well, yes, I am psychoanalytically-oriented and therefore this is what I think.

If the lawyers do not really have the ability to probe those kinds of systems, you will never understand what it is that they are recommending, anyhow. And if they did understand what they were recommending, they would find out it has absolutely no validity. I mean, Dr. Leslie Drozd is trying to do something which I think is very interesting, and that is to really—I do not want to use the word "codify"—but certainly standardize some ways in how you can come to decisions more objectively.

My only problem persists after being a professional for the number of years that I have, which is pretty much the 40 years of experience we all have or approach here. The word "objective" is abusive because it abuses reality. The fact remains this is an ultimately subjective decision that we make. It is based upon these subjective, not objective factors. We can cook it up and we can dress it up, but, you know the old saying that if you put lipstick on the pig, it is still, you know, it is still a pig, whether it looks good or not.

And while I do think we can get to a point as Dr. Andrew Benjamin is trying to get there, and I would certainly go in Andy's direction—but Andy's direction is not psychological. If you listen to what Andy was saying, it's legal. It's actually legal. Well, why shouldn't the judges and the attorneys be doing it? Why is it that psychologists should be doing it?

And so I think that, if we are going to evolve towards a better system, which we all admit is broken, we also have to admit what our real limitations are. I just think that there is so much abuse in the mental health field that ultimately if we do not take a stand on that, the number of people that are being harmed by that is just exponentially growing, and we will never get a grip on that unless we accept that as professionals we have an unbelievable amount of limitations. We should not try to project that we know something that we don't. And you see that in court and in forensic work day in and day out.

SECOND AUDIENCE SPEAKER: Okay. But my question was how to reconcile one set of comments, which is that the practice is substandard and leads to bad outcomes, and other propositions of actually there's ways to have better practice. And, so, the people who are saying the practice is substandard are saying, "Throw the bums out," and then others are saying, "Yes, but don't go right now."

UNIDENTIFIED PANEL SPEAKER: Actually, your question, I think, is relevant to this discussion.

I think there is a really fundamental problem in everything we have talked about today, and the fundamental problem is that we are working in a system that Toby Kleinman characterizes as a search for truth. It's not. It is a search for closure. And all of our efforts are attempts to sort of come closer and closer to a truth, but the reality is that what we can contribute, as psychologists, as lawyers, as doctors, isn't closure. It is an approximation, which through cross-validation, through the tools of science, of training, can get us closer and closer to something that we might agree, we might concur looks like something that approximates a truth which we can never really grasp, because we cannot grasp—we cannot plumb human behavior to that extent with our tests and our interviews and our training in human behavior.

And so I would suggest a very different approach, which is a recognition of error, and the acknowledgment of error, that we aren't ever going to get truth. We are going to try to have closure because we have a court system that requires it—there is going to be a closure. And there are two big gaps in that truth-to-closure closing. The first big gap is that there is error; however, we are going to try and define human behavior and understand human behavior. Then the second big gap is that there is a judge who has to make a decision. And the judge is making a decision on the erroneous assumption that he or she can come to a truthful closure. And so I think we should begin to look more carefully at the least detrimental errors in our understanding of the impacts of our evaluations on children, rather than what is going to—like infinity—you know, you never quite get to the end of it because—you know, I don't know-pi—or whatever it is, we need to look at error. And then we need to look at what are the implications of Error A versus Error B and to educate the court not just on, well, this is what the truth is and you have this person saying this is the truth and that person saying that is the truth, but rather saying, you know, Your Honor, we will never have a sure truth here because a sure truth is unobtainable. So we can look at the probabilities that are, and argue for our view being closer to the truth, but then you have basically a decision in which there are two possibilities for error: the error that takes this way of looking at it or the error that takes this way of looking at it.

And then I think one of the ways that we can close this gap, the gap between reality and certainty and decision, is by looking at the effects of error on the child and educating the court about the implications for each kind of error on outcomes for the child. So if your error, to put it very plainly, has to do with whether a child has been sexually abused, you have the choice of believing whatever the sources are, the accusation or allegations, or believing whatever the denials are about that allegation, then you can ask the court: What would be the effects on the child if the sexual abuse happened or of making the error of believing the denials and what would be the effects on the child if the sexual abuse didn't happen of believing the allegation that it did, and which is the more acceptable error?

DR. JANET CUMMINGS: I am aware that we are past time, so I am going to go ahead and dismiss those who wish to be dismissed. I will also ask our presenters to remain for a few more pending questions.

THIRD AUDIENCE SPEAKER: I feel one of the crises in family court is that we are not putting the goal to protect the children. That should be the goal and the target: protect the children. And talking to judges, I guess it's against the law to do that.

But I wanted to especially point out that Child Protective Services' unsubstantiated findings of abuse are not the same as false allegations, yet warrant divorce court to award abusive parents custody. Under the scrutiny of Los Angeles County Child Protective Services—

DR. JANET CUMMINGS: Ma'am, excuse me. We have asked that you address your questions individually to our presenters and not to the wider audience at this point. We actually have the gentleman who was ahead of you in asking questions. Thank you.

FOURTH AUDIENCE SPEAKER: Thanks for a very great series of speakers. It has been thoroughly thought-provoking and headache-causing. I read a little piece in Judge Fields' paper, a statement that I am not quoting exactly, that there is little or no evidence of effective batterer interventions.

Just very, very quickly: Is there anything that says we should support that? I am from New Mexico where now it is that domestic violence programs who are offering batterers intervention programs, they are mandated across the state to provide 12-month periods, and I do not know whether—my theory is that more of the same does not produce any better results. So just thoughts about that?

DR. SHAPIRO: Yeah, just very briefly, you are absolutely right. There is no good evidence that the batterers' treatment programs as they are currently constituted are at all effective. From my review of them, one of the problems is, they are doing exactly what I said we should not be doing, which is, one size fits all. Everyone is going into these psycho-educational groups regardless of whether their battering is due to the power and control, which is what most of them are, whether they are mentally ill batterers, whether they are substance-abusing batterers. It is like they are all being treated the same. And I think that that is why the outcome data are so terrible. That if you are going to have batterer treatment programs, then they have to address what kind of batterer it is you are dealing with.

DR. CACCAVALE: I was under the impression for a long period of time that the best program for batterers is jail. So, you know, it seemed to me that—at least from my own experience and the research that I have seen over the years—is that if a woman called the cops when she was battered and the husband even for one night was put in jail, that tended to reduce future episodes. Well, I don't mean for one night. What I am saying is that jail seems to be a good deterrent because, you know, if you put the person away and I—well, it stops the violence from that person. I mean, one of the things that Judge Marjory Fields said, which I thought was very, very important, was that.

FOURTH AUDIENCE SPEAKER: Good. Then that's it.

DR. WALKER: Well, there are some data. We can talk about our impressions and our feelings, but being a psychologist I always go back to the data. The data are not good in terms of what we would like batterers to do, which is to totally stop their violent behavior and stop their abuse of power and control. They sort of fall out about a third, a third, and a third, meaning about a third of them, when they go into the batterer intervention program, they may stop their physical abuse while they are in the program. We know nothing about whether they stop their sexual abuse or not. And we know that from the data that they increase their psychological coercive power and control behavior. And when we put them in jail, we know the same thing happens about their psychological coercive power and control behavior because who are they learning from but the other people who are committing criminal acts in jails and in prisons. And so if we really want to deter them, we have to put them in prison forever, just lock them up forever, and that is not going to happen and probably should not happen except for a small percentage who really should not be out. And those people we are pretty good at picking them out and arresting them and prosecuting them and having them in jails and prisons.

However, we talked about reality, and reality and budget cuts tell us that a lot of them are being sent back out into the community because of the expense of keeping them locked up. So we would be far better off, in my opinion, of finding the ways of trying to prevent them in the first place, or at least when we begin to see the signs of bullying behavior in children, in the teenagers that have been so exposed to violence and abuse, that we need to get into the detention centers and do some interventions there and work with community-based programs where we might have a chance of stopping this kind of behavior as they are growing up. If we do not do that, then we will be left with spending a lot more money on the other end.

DR. JANET CUMMINGS: I am told that we need to close, so we will take one last question of the woman standing at this point.

FIFTH AUDIENCE SPEAKER: The question I have is: You know, I have heard some really heinous crimes described today against children, the anal penetration, you know, some of the things that make us gasp. If this happened to any one of us walking down the street and there was no gender involved and we were not under the protection of a family unit or the family court or even Child Protective Services to be working—you know, thinking about what we want to do, what is the law, just the law about any one of these heinous crimes being inflicted on any one of us? Let's say we aren't even going to put gender into this, just to find out what is the law.

UNIDENTIFIED PANEL SPEAKER: Well, first of all, laws vary from state to state, but the procedure would be entirely different. How someone gets charged would be up to either a district attorney or a prosecuting attorney. It would be referred to them, but basically it is a different procedure, and different standards apply. In my opinion, as I said before, they shouldn't apply.

FIFTH AUDIENCE SPEAKER: So my final question then—you don't have to answer it—is why are we putting up with this?

PREVIOUS UNIDENTIFIED PANEL SPEAKER: For all the reasons we have been talking about.

FIFTH AUDIENCE SPEAKER: Oh, well, there you go, the broken family court.

DR. JANET CUMMINGS: On that final note, this concludes the extended panel discussion, with the reminder that there will be a closing panel in which possible future directions will be discussed.

Chapter 15

The Better Use of the Criminal Court By Family Court Judges

Robert Adler, J.D.

DR. JANET CUMMINGS: Our next speaker is Robert Adler. He is a partner at Adler & Kleinman Law with Toby Kleinman. The two are longtime childhood friends, spouses, and law partners, so what an awesome couple. His focus is on family law in cases of child abuse and domestic violence. Mr. Adler was formerly a criminal defense attorney and a civil rights attorney. He uses criminal law to hold abusers responsible for their violence behaviors, and we have been talking a lot about how that is not done. We are going to hear some solutions on how that can be done.

Mr. Adler is a past vice president of the Center for the Protection of Children, which unfortunately no longer exists due to, I guess, budget problems that are affecting a number of organizations. Mr. Adler uses the Constitution to protect children and battered women and has actually gone up against state agencies to enforce the constitutional rights of victims. So please welcome Bob Adler.

ATTORNEY ROBERT ADLER: Thank you, Janet.

You know, as I heard the previous presentations, I believe that Ginger and Toby and Eli with your comments, and along with Marjory, you have said it all. But these issues are so important, at the risk of saying it again, I will go through with my presentation which dovetails into these topics so neatly.

I want to comment at the beginning that if these changes that we all seek did not involve empowering women, it seems to me they would be universally accepted in the country as law and order issues. As has been said at the conference—oh, I have an applause sign [applause]—thank you! As has been said at the conference in many ways, I feel like I am preaching to the choir as so many here today appreciate and have deep concerns for the lack of protection actually given to mothers who suffer violence at home and, as importantly, the lack of protection for their children who witness abuse or are otherwise abused emotionally, physically, and sexually.

The concerns that have been expressed are well-founded. One major problem as expressed by Toby is the failure to implement existing state legislation, which specifically places the safety and risk of safety for the child of paramount concern. The overarching issues range from failures of training and education for judges who hear these matters or court personnel and mental health professionals who are affiliated with the courts, as well as independent evaluators who are asked by the courts to become involved in decision-making when issues of child protection are raised in the court. And the reasons for this range from a value system that varies as to how it determines abuse to lack of resources, shortage of time, demands of individuals' jobs.

As Toby discussed, a change in the lens we use to understand and address child abuse underpins all of these reasons.

There are three typical ways child abuse issues can be presented to the court. Usually it is presented in a matrimonial court by a parent who learns of the abuse during the pendency of a divorce proceeding. These are also brought in by a state agency who hears of the child's abuse and makes a fact-finding of abuse as founded and actually uses the state protective child safety and protection statute to file a complaint against the abuser.

Lastly, a parent in many states can file using the same child protection statute that the CPS agencies use, and as you heard, it is available in New Jersey where I work. We have used it successfully and it is available in about 15 other jurisdictions. I might point out here that the Massachusetts domestic violence statute also allows a victim of domestic violence to file her own criminal complaint. It is a great model, and I recommend it and reference it for people who are looking for ideas as to what to include in a domestic violence statute.

Ways in which Child Protection Is Undermined

Despite the state laws providing that child protection shall have the highest priority in the law, child safety actually gets lost in the other business of court. When the issue is merged into a divorce, the child safety issue is just one more of the issues the parties have to resolve, and, as noted most often, the child goes unrepresented. If the state agency charged with protecting the children disagrees with you with respect to whether the child needs protection for whatever reason, they often become an adversary in the issue of child protection. And you find you not only have your own burden of filing the case, but the Child Protection Service agency is in it to justify their lack of action in the case. Instead of helping you, they undermine your case. Even in a case where the state agency believes the child is the victim of a crime, their case has its own legs. They control the nature of protection sought, and because of dual mandates, largely, and other discretionary considerations, they may take the case from one slap on the wrist in the defender to the next slap on the wrist and the next slap on the wrist, while abusers continue through either direct contact, violation of court orders, or other threat—financial or other controls—to continue the abuse; in a sense, converting the original power and control into litigation abuse.

The things these methods or courts have in common is that, with the cultural changes we all hope will occur, the court will have to believe the protective parent, usually the mother, and today the mother is generally disbelieved. Allegations of child abuse today are viewed as just another arrow in a hateful woman's quiver. They look at what she has done and they say: Look, she will stop at nothing.

So the current system with three separate courts that are capable and usually do hear child abuse, the system is still not working. Some of the speakers pointed to the fact that to make child protection the highest priority in a judicial scheme, it would require revamping social and cultural notions of our ways of thinking about children: abuse, women, or other assumptions that we hold dear; among others, the importance of a unified family or even the importance of parental contact. Even if you could get the perfect judge who appears no-nonsense at the beginning and you have credentialed experts and assume you have specially trained judges, qualified mental health evaluators, and social worker investigators and responsive police action, there still seems in the course of this litigation to be a tipping point, at which some of these and then others involved pull back from the original issue, which was child protection, and implement them in plain words of the legislation. And it does a complete turn of the tables, and the party raising the issue becomes the suspect rather than pointing a finger at the accused parent. In each of these three typical circumstances to protect the child, the parent becomes a difficult and unbelievable, hostile person who is so angry and that she is using the courts to take out her rage against the other. And this initially protective parent gets called the uncooperative parent, the one who will not accept the recommended settlement on the issues of contact, the one who is too angry to share joint custody, possibly so far out there she should have no contact at all. Lenore presented just frightening statistics that are out there: 50% of the protective parents who raise child abuse lose custody. They lose more than custody. They do not even have supervised visitation. They end up with a "no contact" order against them. This happens every day of the week in cases one by one across the country.

The Abuser Gets Protected

Most of the time you cannot get the child agency investigative report through issues of disclosure. And child safety court proceedings are sealed. Even the proceedings in the divorce case can be selectively sealed, all ostensibly to protect the child. Who do you think gets protected? It is the abuser and it is the state agency that is involved. This is the typical setting and it needs to be shaken up. A change in the commitment of a community needs to occur from the police officer on the beat all the way up to the judge. I recommend that from now on and forever you call the violence upon a child a crime, not merely child abuse, but the crime of child abuse. Go directly to the police to report a crime. Make a record of that specific report. Mandated reports must, and mandated reporters must also report to CPS, and in return they should refer it to a prosecutor. You can call the prosecutor. You can go directly to the sex crime unit of the prosecutor's office. In the absence of a confession or compelling circumstantial evidence case, a criminal case is harder to take to ultimate conviction, and the prosecutor still has the almighty power of discretion. They make policy decisions, and public opinion does not generally support criminally charging a child's parent absent a public outcry in an individual case. The burden of proof in a criminal case is greater, beyond a reasonable doubt. The child victim would probably have to withstand confrontation and cross-examination. The prosecutor may evaluate the protective parent as weak or incredible. Obviously, with discretion, there is an area where old-fashioned bias against women can surface: a failure to charge, risks appearing, like a statement of support or commitment to the abuser, and all future abusers.

I would like to see a decision in the community to take every criminal act against a child directly to a criminal court and let the court set the example for the entire community that child abuse is criminal and there is a zero tolerance for it in your community.

Involving the Criminal Justice System

The need for more involvement of the criminal justice system—criminal courts, the prosecutor's office, as well as sheriffs' and police departments and investigation and enforcement of child protection—is one major area that is fertile ground in a fight to save children from abuse. Indeed, it should be required.

So how do we use the criminal justice system to beef up child protection? And to also empower the protective parent instead of impaling them. As all of you probably know by now, family courts are an island unto themselves. They seem to shoot from the hip and go by cowboy rules. Whatever seems okay at the time gets fitted into the rules that do exist. There are always ways, however, to stop the lawlessness of family court. The ways require actually following the letter of the law as well as the spirit of the law as it is written. It requires the initial recognition that where a child makes a disclosure it is potentially a crime committed against a child, stated by the child. It is a crime that as a society we find intolerable when committed by strangers. Our criminal courts are designed to handle this crime. We do not require victims of robberies to be evaluated. We do not require victims of home break-ins to be evaluated. Prosecutors or a district attorney, they hear what they say happened to them, and they look at the evidence. The model generally works. But so often prosecutors do not prosecute crimes of child abuse for many reasons, including children have been evaluated in family court over and over, over-evaluated, and disbelieved by unqualified or untrained or unscrupulous evaluators. If what we know about these sex crimes were integrated into a policy decision, then these perpetrators could be prosecuted. For example, children disclose to people they trust. They disclose details over time. There is much research about how children disclose abuse and to whom. It should be utilized.

So assuming we want to protect women from violence in their homes by their spouse or boyfriend or former spouse, and we want to protect children to assure them safety in their homes, what do we do? And then how can a family court be simpatico with the criminal court? And here I propose where, in Cummings County, if a parent brings a child's outcry of abuse to family court, all contact with the named perpetrator should stop, pending the prosecutor's investigation of the case. Or when any family court judge is apprised of a disclosure about abuse or a spouse abuse or hears from a credentialed expert that abuse exists, it must send the matter of child abuse or spouse abuse to a prosecutor, not to an evaluator. In either of these circumstances, the prosecutor must examine whether or not probable cause exists and believe a crime has been committed, using the same standards used every day in making charging decisions and following through when probable cause is established through indictment or criminal complaint and preliminary hearing. As prosecutors have broad discretion with respect to whether to indict or charge an abuser and make these pro or con decisions for reasons that may have nothing to do with his belief that a crime is committed, a prosecutor's decision may be based upon his belief that he cannot prove his case beyond a reasonable doubt, for one example, his assessment of witnesses, a decision with respect to the strength of the child witness, his assessment of the protective parent, and his recognition of court resources, or a belief that his office cannot afford to prosecute.

Probable Cause

Whatever his decision, he should place it in writing. He should state whether or not there was probable cause to believe a crime was committed in his opinion and state the reasons they have not taken the case for prosecution. If probable cause is believed by the prosecutor, a decision not to charge for any reason whatsoever, the case will get transferred back to family court where a civil hearing on child abuse or spouse abuse must take place. In other words, there will be no custody hearings until there is a full evidentiary hearing on the child abuse/spouse abuse issue through proper evidentiary standards and using only battered women's experts and child abuse experts, not custody evaluators.

In all circumstances where an evaluator has been hired by a parent or the child's doctor's referral, or a child's doctor, these expert opinions will get the same weight as any court-appointed evaluator would have had in a civil or criminal hearing. Moreover, there would be no court-appointed evaluation if there is probable cause, as the prosecutor's investigatory team will be required to come over and testify in the civil case. A "no contact" order with the main perpetrator, as with stranger violence, must continue through criminal or civil hearing once there is a finding of probable cause to believe a crime occurred. And it cannot be modified until conclusion. At no time after probable cause is found should the perpetrator be considered to be a potential custodian on the issue of changes as to whether or not there should be any contact once the matter is returned to family court.

This is true of both spouse abuse and child abuse crimes. The protective parent's voice will be given deference as to how contact will occur, if at all, and the protective parent will not have her parental rights—and I say "her." It is usually the women, although I have represented battered men. They exist, but they are not part of the everyday model we see most of the time.

The Rights of the Protective Parent and the Child

The court is not going to keep control of the protective parent and tell her what doctors she may use or what therapist she can use for the health of the child. These are decisions she is left to be able to make without the interference of the court. A decision not to prosecute should have no negative evidentiary value in a child protection case where the standards are either a preponderance or by clear and convincing evidence. Standards below that are criminal prosecution. There shall be no negative inference to the parent who brought the abuse issue in front of the court. Even where a prosecutor finds no probable cause, that finding cannot be used against the parent who raised the issue, and the matter goes back to family court for resolution.

All children will have their own attorney and will be appointed as soon as the issue arises regardless of who raises it. The attorney for the child will be from the Division of Sex Crimes Unit preferably. They are in the business of prosecuting cases. We need the prosecutor to have an investment in women. These attorneys will be appointed in every case where child abuse is raised as an issue. The child then gets a seat at the table. He gets to approve any settlement, examine and cross-examine witnesses, argue before the trial court, and prosecute an appeal for any violation of his rights as a citizen entitled to state protection.

If there is a prosecution of the offender, the protective parent's request to relocate or to move should be readily considered and granted. Let her move to secure the safety of the child, and their own enjoyment of life should be permitted in the civil courts. Let them move where there is work, where there is family. Instead of treating her as a vicious intermeddler in the other parent's rights to contact with the child, she should be applauded for having made the emotional and practically difficult decision to go to court for child protection and to be allowed to get away or out from under abuser control, away from litigation and harassment during the pendency of the case and empower, not impale, the parent victim.

Be prepared to give victim compensation funds to the victims of abuse as financial issues continue, and often the breadwinner is now in jail. Domestic violence protective orders must be entered against all perpetrators, and all violations must be prosecuted. There are no small violations of domestic violence protective orders in the eyes of the abused person. Violations should equal mandatory jail time. Let it be known in your jurisdiction there is a zero tolerance for violations of temporary or permanent restraining orders. If there is a conviction in the criminal courts of sex abuse or spouse abuse crime, even with no jail time, or after jail, a "no contact" order must be continued so long as the protective parent believes it is in the child's interests to do so. It is easier and quicker to revoke probation and/or parole in the case of longer incarceration. And this can be done readily in the criminal court.

Dealing seriously with criminals who happen to be parents and having a zero tolerance for violations of protective orders will give all of the relevant support staff--from the sheriff's office to the local police department and into the prosecutor's office—the additional will to carry out their part in this new culture.

Is this an "applause" sign? [Applause.]

At a civil trial, if the child's safety evidentiary hearing is at a civil trial, the child's words through others are an exception to the hearsay rule. They will reconsider evidence, but there should not be a finding of abuse on the child's hearsay words alone, absent the child's own testimony. If the child does not testify and only his words are used, the abuse must be corroborated in some other fashion: expert report, factualized behavior, age inappropriate behavior, bruises, or other permissible evidence. Hopefully, a community commitment to address these crimes and in this manner will help protect abused children and/or protect the parent, albeit one case at a time.

Thank you.

Chapter 16
No Way Out But One

Garland Waller

DR. JANET CUMMINGS: Garland Waller is currently an Assistant Professor in the Department of Television and Film at Boston University. She has used her filmmaking talents for social causes, not just for all the reasons we surf many channels on TV, trying to find something decent and interesting to watch. She is producing more than films on timely, interesting topics. She uses her films to make a difference.

One of her previous films was *Small Justice, Little Justice in America's Family Courts.* She also did a film debating Richard Gardner, where she exposed the lack of scientific basis for his theories about parental alienation syndrome, unlock syndrome, which was discussed quite a bit with a number of the speakers.

We are going to ask Garland to talk a little bit about her newest film, and then we will have the premier showing of *No Way Out But One.* It is a very, very moving film, depicting the length that some mothers will go to and have gone to so as to protect their children in a system that does not protect its children. Even though this is the premier showing, some of the speakers and organizers got to view the film ahead of time, and I can attest that it is extremely well worth seeing. So welcome Garland Waller.

PROFESSOR GARLAND WALLER: Thank you very much. I am really happy to be here.

Whenever I speak, I write a speech and usually somehow I end up putting it aside as soon as I get up in front of people. My ex-husband found this irritating. My current husband finds it charming. So I am sticking with the one who finds me charming. Thank you, thank you, thank you.

There are several people that I want to be sure and thank. One of them is not in the room, so I am going to wait just a little bit to thank her, but speaking of my husband, I just want to give him credit right at the very beginning because one of the reasons that this documentary ended up getting made is because my husband, whose name is Barry Noland, which will be a familiar name to some of you—you will have seen or heard him on TV—really said, "You need to do this." He encouraged me to do it. Now, here is why I am speaking today, and here is how this setup is going to be. I am going to speak for 20 minutes, we are going to show the documentary, which is a feature-length documentary at 1½ hours, and then after that, there will be 10 minutes for questions. But the talk part, the introduction part, of what I am about to do has to do with the extreme failure of the mainstream media to cover this issue.

The reason why you are seeing an independent, low-budget documentary on this issue is because mainstream media will not do this issue. And there are a number of reasons why they won't.

Now, in a previous chapter and in a different venue I wrote what I called *The Yuck Factor*, which is part of a book on domestic violence and child custody that is published by the Civic Research Institute, I wrote several reasons why I believed there was a problem with the mainstream media, why they wouldn't cover these issues and what we had to do about it.

Now, what I want to also mention is, there is a simple story here that the mainstream media can't get. And, by the way, I consider the mainstream media just as guilty as the family courts for not protecting children, absolutely 100%, and until the media begins to really understand, and possibly until we hold their feet to the fire, we will not be able to make the changes that are necessary to be made. But the question that—when I talk to the media—because very often I am trying to get them to do stories on this issue—I say to them, "This is an issue that has to do with batterers getting custody of children. This is not an issue about divorce. It is not even an issue just about custody. It is about a very narrow group of people that beat people up and rape them that get custody." Now, what I will also say to you is this: The reporters get real interested in that. "Hot dog! Hot dog, we have got sex and violence; we're on a roll."

What happens, I believe, is that stories get produced. Before they can go on the air, they have to be really vetted by the legal department at any television, radio, media outlet, et al., and once the legal department gets a whiff of this issue, the show dies. Now, I am going to name names. ABC went to Chicago to cover the story that we heard about: Crystel Strileoff, $25 million bond. This was a horrific case. Helen has been here talking—mentioning a little bit about it—it was a horrific case, with tons of evidence of violent sexual abuse of the children. It is too complicated. I am not going to tell you the story here. Long story short: Chris Cuomo, ABC, went and spent, I think about a week, covering the story, doing the story for ABC. ABC also went and shot the Holly Collins story, which is what you are going to see today. They did not put it on the air. The reporters are committed, but the legal department is terrified. And the legal department is terrified because they hear a couple of things. He-said-she-said, that's all they really hear. And they hear the very loud fathers' rights groups who shout and who say, "I will sue you if you put this on the air." And the networks, the media back down. So we have got a huge, huge problem with exposure.

Now, I am going to have to look at my notes again, because, as I said, I went off message. But one of the things that I want to talk about today is both how victims and how advocates can talk to the press. And the other thing I want to talk about is some of these other issues that keep the press from covering the stories.

Why the Press Will Not Cover the Stories

Now, here is the first reason the press won't cover the stories. They are disgusting. Six o'clock news, even 20/20, on those shows, it is still disgusting to talk about raping babies. It is still disgusting to talk about beating babies up. My own particular feeling is, there is a special place in hell—not purgatory, because I do not think they will ever get out of purgatory—for people who beat up children and rape them. But that is a horse of a different color. Okay. The stories are disgusting. People do not want to read them. People do not want to read or see these stories in the press unless there is a celebrity attached. Now, I think that this is really significant. The stories that you have heard are Mel Gibson, are Jon Binet Ramsey. The reason Mel Gibson got so much press is because he is a celebrity. And Jon Binet Ramsey was young and pretty and blonde. So being pretty and blonde helps a lot. That helps with exposure. This is a comment that shows how entertainment-oriented the press is. Now, I happen to believe that old adage:

The press belongs to anybody—I'm stealing the line—the press belongs to anybody who can afford to buy one. And I think that is really true, and I think we are seeing our political institutions that are owned or controlled by money, and I think we have to understand that the media are owned. There is a board of directors. There are stockholders. This is about money. So if your show, if your story is not going to make them money, they don't want to do the story. And here is what makes it complicated. If it is a complicated story, it is going to take resources; it is going to take time; it is going to take talking to both sides. Now, that is another aside.

Fathers' rights groups and fathers now understand how to stop the story, and the way to stop the story is not to talk to the press, because the press wants both sides. So it is a cement wall that is very real, very real. So that is one thing: The stories are complicated.

And here is the other thing that is hard. The stories don't end. They go on forever. On TV, people want a beginning, middle, and end. They want it to end. They want to dust themselves off and say, "All done." And you can't do these with these complicated stories. Earlier in the day, we heard some people talking about New York and different states and different laws and different rules. There was a very small story in the *New York Times* about a reporter, a *New York Times* reporter, who went to try to get into the family court, several family courts, in New York, and he was booted out. Now, this wasn't years ago. This was about three months ago. And he wrote about it. And I immediately wrote to him and said, "Don't drop this story. You are sitting on a Pulitzer. Don't drop it." Well, they dropped it, which shows you my sway in the mainstream media world.

But what was really important to me was that it was yet another story, for we had the Jerry Sandusky story, we had the Powell story, and we have had all of these individual stories. We have the Catholic priest scandal, and one of the problems that we are facing in this world of the people who are knowledgeable about this issue is: I believe our mandate has to be context. Bob Adler talked about the tipping point. Well, there is a big book called *The Tipping Point*, and the tipping point really is, at a certain point, there is going to be so much information that they can't ignore it anymore, that the system has to change.

Now, I do believe that sunlight is the best disinfectant, and I do believe that change is going to only come when the family courts are exposed and when the media begin to take some bold steps. Now, here are some of the things that I think we really need to do as we think about how to try to convince the media to do some of these stories.

One is, when women and advocates begin to call up a reporter, they begin with, first there were the dinosaurs. My experience with women and advocates who have been going through this issue, trying to get this issue exposed, is they start 10 years ago, and until they learn how to summarize years of pain and trauma in the family court in 30 seconds, they are not going to get anywhere. I am not saying it is right. I am saying that is how the system works. And so they have got to learn to start with the worst part first. Then the next thing they have to say is, "I am one-thousandth thousandths of the women and children in this country that this is happening to. And until people put this in context of the numbers, we are going to stay with each woman having the worst story that has ever been told in the whole world, and you will get nowhere. So everybody has got to really figure out that there has got to be a new system. There has got to be a new way to talk about this.

We need to help the press understand that batterers are more likely than non-batterers to get custody. We need short, sweet, sail-this-little-sucker-right-out sound bites, sound bites that they can remember. If they don't have those, if you have got to explain it in 10 minutes or more, forget it. So we also need to put this in context of divorce in general. And by that I mean what I was saying at the very beginning, which is, this is not about most divorce cases. In most divorce cases, even if people hate each other, they figure out what is best for the kids. This is about the small group of people that beat and rape other people.

Now, I am going to say a couple of more things. Andrew Vachss is noted for—or not noted—for saying, one of the biggest problems that we have right now in general is that pedophiles have learned to grow their own victims. And I believe that is something that advocates and people who work in this business need to understand. There is a new rule, and it was—we heard Toby Kleinman speak and Bob Adler speak, and several other people speak—we heard it, that we have to present this as a crime, and it's a crime. But pedophiles can hurt their own children. If you rape a stranger, you will go to jail. If you rape your child, you get custody of your child. Now, pedophiles know this. That is why you are seeing more men marry women with young children and then suddenly they go after the women's children in a custody case. So, I am just going to leave you with some uncomfortable thoughts.

I want to very specifically thank the woman who somebody called a pit bull, and I'm with you. I have not seen any pit bull, but the reason that that *No Way Out But One* was able to be a documentary that exists today is because of Toby Kleinman. Tom Cruise in one of his films said, "Show me the money." She said, because this would have taken years if we had had to go through grant-making organizations, we must get individuals to contribute. So God bless you, Toby Kleinman, you got individuals to contribute the money.

The last thing I am going to say before we show the documentary is this: I want you to hear my pitch, the pitch that I use when I talk to TV people or news people, because I work very hard to sum up a whole documentary in proper context. *No Way Out But One* is an independent documentary on the first American woman to be granted asylum by the Dutch government on grounds of domestic violence. That is the sentence. Every story needs a sentence like that when you are talking to the press, every story. If you want to go on and on and on, they're not listening. Trust me; they're not listening. That is the pitch. That is what we sell.

Now, I want to say one more thing, because I mentioned it earlier. This Pulitzer thing, I really believe that when you talk to the press—and I believe we should all be talking to the press—I think we should just be bugging them all the time about doing stories on this. I think it is okay to say, "You know, this is a Pulitzer Prize winning story if you do it right. I heard an expert say it was a Pulitzer Prize winning story." I'm the expert. You heard it. So, I say this because I really do believe they are motivated by goodwill. I believe they are motivated by getting awards and making money and getting rated. I would like to tell you after all these years that I still believe in the nobility of the press, but I do not believe that anymore. But I do believe that we must get this story out. So this independent documentary is an independent documentary that, God willing, will get on the air. But if it doesn't, please spread the word. So we will watch *No Way Out But One* now, and then Toby and I will be able to answer questions when it is over if you have any questions. Thank you.

[Movie viewed. The reader can obtain a disc of the film at modest cost for its reproduction. Contact The Cummings Foundation, 4781 Caughlin Parkway, Reno, Nevada 89519.]

PROFESSOR WALLER: I am working very hard to get this into festivals and to get a buzz going. So one of the things that I would ask here is for you all to talk about it, to go to our website, our Facebook page, so that we can start to build a buzz. And I would accept contributions, absolutely, because the next thing we have really got to do is raise some money. I mean, we really literally do not have any more money even to enter into film festivals at this point. However, just yesterday—I learned and forgot to tell you, that I got an email from my husband saying that *No Way Out One But* has been selected for an Accolade Award, so that is wonderful. And last week it was selected for the Bare Bones Film Festival in Muskogee, Oklahoma.

So since I don't believe anymore that the mainstream press is going to sort of tap me on the shoulder and say, "Oh, great work. Come on, Babe." I don't think that is going to happen. I think there is going to have to be a groundswell of demand, and I think it may be from the Internet or—but we don't have our marketing plan down yet. We're working on it. That's next. Oh. Kathleen?

JUDGE KATHLEEN: Thank you for this incredible contribution to the movement, and I also want to follow up in terms of what people can do with this film, because the Center for Judicial Excellence has rented a theatre in California to view the premier of this film in our community, and anyone in this room, particularly if you are involved with a social service agency, a domestic violence shelter, any organization that has any resources, we are going to be charging admission at the door in hope that it might actually be a fundraiser for our organization, which Garland has been very supportive of being able to use this film to tell this story beyond the choir that is in this room. We really need to reach into the hearts and minds of regular good-ole people whose lives haven't been devastated in the family courts. And every time we do that, we convert people, and they say, "What can I do? How can I help?" And they warn their friends before they go to family court. So this is an incredible tool for community education and for creating the political will that we need to create to bring about change. So we plan to use this film to continue to do the advocacy that is so necessary politically as well as with the media. We are hoping to get some local reporters to come to the film and to write about it, because Holly is just one of millions of parents and many—I know here in the room—are living this nightmare, and hopefully this film will tell everyone's story. So thank you.

PROFESSOR GARLAND: Thank you, Kathleen. Thank you.

ANOTHER JUDGE SPEAKER: Before the film, Dr. Newberger mentioned with regard to Dr. Felitti and Kaiser Permanente and the ACE study, that there is a film that was done related from the human rights vantage point from, you know, a trauma vantage point called *Healing Neen*. It won an award out of Sundance. It is also a feature film. It runs just about under an hour. It is amazing, just like this film, amazing. What the filmmakers did in *Healing Neen* is they went ahead, and made a personal choice—I don't know how that process happens—but they decided to go ahead and put it on the Internet so that anybody could access it full length, no fee. It was—Video-something? Does anybody know that site? Videocom—Anyway, *Healing Neen* is the name, but that is not my point.

My point is that, what I did, as soon as I found out about it, I took it and I emailed it to every single one of our judges in my jurisdiction. And, I mean, I would love to do the same thing with this film, because it is shocking. I have been on the bench 15 years, and, believe me, there is a chasm between the criminal bench, for example, and this bench, and we don't know what is happening. I have never practiced family law. It is shocking. It is a disgrace, and if I see my brother in and sister in, I am going to ask them if they are aware of this film, that they must watch it, and I do think peer pressure, even from other judges, is significantly valuable. So if you can please check out *Healing Neen*, that might be one pathway to creating that buzz. Thank you.

PROFESSOR WALLER: We welcome all ideas. We're looking.

MALE SPEAKER: Thanks for this. It is incredible.

I would like to make people aware, if you are interested in places where you can talk and speak about this kind of thing. I want to tell you, in New Mexico where I am from, we have one of the largest conferences devoted to similar issues. It is called the Children's Law Institute and it is sponsored by the University of

New Mexico's School of Law. I have had the privilege of presenting there on a number of issues that we are doing in my county on occasions, and it is an incredibly vibrant and a far-reaching conference. We have usually over 600 to 700 people that attend that conference, and never has this issue been raised there, although lots of other child welfare kinds of things are there constantly. It is made up equally of the child welfare system personnel and the legal system personnel. I am going to take all of this information and supply it to those people who I know that are part of that Children's Law Institute. But if you are looking for venues, they send out requests for proposals.

PROFESSOR WALLER: This would be wonderful.

MALE SPEAKER: Yes.

PROFESSOR WALLER: This would be a terrific opportunity.

MALE SPEAKER: This would be an incredible thing to show, so I am going to pass this along, and I will get you in touch with the people that I know that are part of that institute. It's a great thing and so good luck with it.

PROFESSOR WALLER: Thank you so much. And I thank all of you as I have been given the time signal. Thank you so much, everybody. I really think this is great. Thank you.

Chapter 17
What Can Be Done About Fixing the Broken Family Court System?

The Closing Panel of Speakers

DR. WALKER: Any of our advocates who want to come up here because this is going to take some advocacy as well, just drag a chair and come on up. And anybody who is willing to move up, it will make it easier for us to see you and for you to grab the microphone as well.

What we really want to talk about is where to go from here. And I will start us off with some positive plans. As you heard earlier when we first started, we have got a video that has been made of all of our talking and our comments, and that video is going to be transcribed and is going to be edited and then put into a book, and that book is going to be distributed to all the policymakers and Congress that Dr. Nick Cummings can find, and he ferrets them out everywhere. So it is going to get into the positive hands that we want it to be in. And now after that very moving story, *No*

Way Out But One, that is now going to be made into a DVD and attached to the book that will go to the Members of Congress. The video will also be available at cost through the Cummings Foundation. And if anybody watches that video, they cannot possibly have a dry eye or not want to be part of the solution.

But we have got to go even further than that, and one of the suggestions that has been made is that we put together a small group of people to go march on Congress and do a congressional briefing, so that we have information into the *Congressional Record,* as a possibility. And another suggestion that has been made, which I think is going to come to fruition, is that we remain as a core group of the people up here who are willing to be part of this core group—but expanded, if we need to, to a think tank that will continue on a monthly basis to at least check in with each other as to the ideas that are being passed around about what we can do. Can we find a Cummings County that is willing to start a trauma-informed family court? We just need one—a child-centered one. We just need one.

So I am going to pass the microphone now and ask my wonderful, wonderful panel. So please, I really hope you give them a round of applause. [Applause.] These folks gave up their time, their weekend at absolutely no pay—nobody got paid for this—to come to share for two days with one another. What a wonderful service that you all have done, and Garland with her fabulous film. You know many of us work tirelessly. I have been in this movement for almost 40 years, and I will share with you one of the things that I learned from the late Andrew Young when he worked on the Civil Rights Movement. He said to me: "You know, the only way that we could keep going was that we have to do three months on and then three months off to recuperate, because if we do not take care of ourselves, we are not going to have the strength to keep going."

And I think we have to really learn that ourselves as well. So I promise as we work, I won't bug you more than once every three months, and then you will have three months off and then we are back again, fighting for the right cause for three more months.

So, I am going to pass the microphone and then I am going to ask everybody up here to give us at least one idea that you have developed over these two days, because these people did not all know each other beforehand. This is the first time everybody has all been together. So one idea that you have developed; and it can be as wild as possible, because nothing is too wild, that you would like to see happen as a result of this conference.

PROFESSOR WALLER: Thank you. You know, my idea came when you just started talking. And I am not as politically involved as a lot of people are, but I am very excited to hear about this book that the Cummings Foundation is going to make sure it gets in the hands of politicians. I am honored that *No Way Out But One* will be part of that.

But in listening to what you just said, I am not so much a believer in marching on Washington, but one of the things I have heard from a lot of people who know a whole more about politics, I would love to see hearings in Washington. And I think that they could be connected to when the book comes out and all that happens, but hearings that would come out and get a celebrity like a George Clooney or like a Reese Witherspoon who is touched by this issue and would be willing to be at the hearing, because, otherwise, there will not be any press. So if you get a celebrity—and I think there really are some—and there is a hearing with expert—experts, I think that there is a way to make this move forward. So that is my mind.

JUDGE LERNER WREN: Well, I guess everybody knows my idea since we started out with it this morning. There is one other thought that I had that I really do believe I had only because I was preparing for this conference. As you know, I am not from the family law sector, but I really do believe that there are fabulously well-informed, humanistic, trauma-informed judges that are out there that are doing really good trauma-informed child-centered work. And if we could try to find one, or two. You know, we could start to showcase them and really hold them up as the standard for other family law judges to aspire to. Judges really do love to be recognized. We are a little narcissistic, it's true. So that is my one thought. So, again, thank you—thank you all very much.

And one other comment: I really heard some wonderful testimony here today from advocates, from real survivors of the family law process, and I just wanted to say I thought you were extraordinary and courageous.

JUDGE AYCOCK: First, I just want to thank you for being invited. This has been wonderful.

A couple of things that we are already in the process of trying to do at the National Council is, we recently received a grant where we are the comprehensive technical assistance providers to state and private court judges on domestic violence, and we are in the planning process with OVW, Office on Violence Against Women, about what exactly that means and what kinds of resources we would have available. You know, connection or website, a link to this kind of material would be great so the judges can see this on a regular basis and read this kind of material.

One of the things that we talked about with OVW was that we are doing this great training. We have done some self-reporting kinds of research with the judges in a pre- and post-survey, and they tell us ahead of time how much they think—do you think you know about domestic violence? Would you say you're a beginner? You're in the middle? You're advanced? You're super? Where are you? Then three to six months later, we ask them, "Now that you have been through the training, and you have been back in your court, where do you think you were before you got here?" Seventy-five percent rate themselves much lower afterwards than they thought they were before. But the problem has been that we train them and then we say "bye" and they go back to their community. We have now got approval from OVW in this grant where we actually are now going to select some of those and actually go out and provide onsite technical assistance around the problems that they are finding in their own court when they get back to their community. So there will be follow-up.

And, Ricky, I wanted to say to you, the judicial guide, we also have a grant to implement that, and we are in the process right now of selecting two sites for an implementation grant where we will also be doing the same thing: We will be going into their communities on a multi-disciplinary level and training around the *Judicial Guide* to *Child Custody* and work on it.

And then on a personal level, one of the things I do is I review our curriculum. We generally do sometimes minor, sometimes major changes on our curriculum. We do our program four times a year, and after every one, we change our curriculum a little bit. We tweak it. We make, like I said, big or little changes. And so one of the things I will be looking for when we are at our next training in April in San Francisco is the lens from this conference, looking at that curriculum as it is actually unfolding in the room and where can we make changes.

The National Council of Juvenile and Family Court Judges is where I work.

DR. WALKER: Thank you. As he is talking, I have got these million things coming in my head, and one of them was, we need a web page.

ATTORNEY ADLER: This institute produces the desk book that the judges use for their own personal custody evaluations. It includes the ideas from APSAC (American Professional Society on the Abuse of Children). It includes procedures that are recommended that are useful from the California studies, from something—I think you have in there from the Affiliated Association of Family Courts, the AAFC. In it, we would recite for the judges in this journal all the time. We photocopy and submit these sections that deal with different areas of forensic evaluation so that the judges are aware that this is not something brand-new in this little case in one corner of the world. This is something that is widespread, thank you for your work.

JUDGE AYCOCK: I can't tell you that we can do that, because I do not make those kinds of decisions for the council. I am the Assistant Director of one of the departments, and so those kinds of decisions get made up there.

JUDGE FIELDS: Since I am a recovering family judge here, I would want family courts to follow the rules of evidence and make decisions based on the law and the legislative intent, and when facts are found, you then grant the remedies that the legislature created and intended for judges to use, and it is just that simple: turn the family court into the court of law that the United States Supreme Court has said repeatedly we have to be—or they have to be. I'm not there anymore.

And that is what would produce different results. If you have evidence of a fractured skull in a child, you cannot as the perpetrator get custody of that child, and you might invite the prosecutor to come into the courtroom and listen to the proceeding to make a decision or send your decision to the prosecutor. I had a case in which the father had sexually abused his two daughters. He also happened to be a public school custodian, and in the course of the case, I turned to the lawyer for the children, and I said— and we have lawyers for children, not guardians *ad litem*—I said, "Counsel, would you send my decision, please, to the Board of Education." And she mumbled something about confidentiality.

No, I sent it, and I got a thank-you letter from the Board of Ed, which was shocking, because usually, you know, you do not get thank-you letters. But he was a risk, and confidentiality was going to leave this pedophile and sex abuser in the school. So there was no criminal conviction, but it certainly rose to the level of requiring an investigation, and on the information we had, it was enough to terminate someone from a position like that. You did not have to have the standard of proof beyond a reasonable doubt, but there was a court file. So those are two things that I would like to see.

And the other is, we have to recognize that much child abuse—and I think I'm right when I say it is only 15% of the cases—where we have physical findings for sexual abuse. Right? Yes. So you are not going to find in a court that you are going to have the medical evidence of child sexual abuse. You have to listen to children and we have to believe children, and it's easy. I think the worst experience I had before I took my seat on the court and I knew I was going to be sworn in was, oh, my God, how am I going to know when they are lying? Well, actually, it is really easy. When they lie, there is a sign that flashes on their forehead. It says: "Lying, lying." Adults think they can get away with it, and what they do is they accuse children of lying. Children lie much less frequently. And adults trip themselves up.

And the other thing judges should do when they write their decisions is make a credibility determination and say why: "I find this witness not credible because he contradicted himself. On Wednesday, he said this and on Friday he said that." That requires listening and taking notes. But that is being a court of law. And that is what the family court should be.

ATTORNEY ADLER: What has come up many times in my mind and in the private discussion with other panel members and other guests that were here is that there is a special circumstance raised when child abuse is raised, and the judge who is hearing it may be on a parallel bench with the family court or the child safety court or civil court. But, in my mind, as soon as there is a child safety issue, the judge really sits in a special role that is different than every other day of the week. Every day of the week they sit there and say, "Show me the evidence. Bring me the evidence." But when they are sitting in *a parens patriae* role for the child, the child is not presenting the evidence, even though the case is brought in the interests of the child. There are no adverse parties. The litigants or the parents are notified because they really should be notified as dispositional parties, but they are not actually parties. It is a judge and a child who needs help and protection. And in light of that, it is my belief that the judge owes a duty to set the standards for the staff to throw out junk science, to tell the mental health professionals, don't bring me reports that are not relevant to the issues that are today before me. Establish the standards for the rules of evidence in the court, without waiting for the child victim to object. He has got to conduct the court to get to the information and set that standard, which will trickle back. He will be shocked when the police don't segregate an abuser from a child. The judge will tell the police what he expects. The judge can tell the mental health investigators what the reports need to do, who to bring in, what is relevant, and what is not relevant, and perhaps act a little bit more forcefully in the course of conducting the trial to protect the child. I see the judge as really the most important participant here when it comes to child protection.

DR. SHAPIRO: In several ways my comments are quite parallel to Bob's. One of the things that horrified me the most in watching Garland Waller's presentation was the absolutely abysmal job that that court evaluator did. And I found myself thinking, you know, what can mental health professionals do to provide higher-quality reports for the courts and to have judges—and this is where it ties into what Bob said—have judges be aware of what is a good quality report and what is garbage, especially since such tremendous kinds of decisions are based on it. As you saw in this video, you know, that she was diagnosed as having Munchausen's, that she was hysterical, she was this, she was that. All she was trying to do was to protect her children.

So one thing I would propose is—you know, we do continuing education for other psychologists, and other mental health professionals. Apparently, it has not worked all that well, because a lot of psychologists are still doing pretty abysmal work. I wonder whether or not providing training seminars, for judges saying this is what a good report looks like; this is what a garbage report looks like, so when the judge gets a garbage report, they recognize it and they can say, "No, I will not accept that." I was talking to Andy before. "Is there some way we can market your comprehensive kinds of evaluations to judges?" So I am going to turn it over to Andy.

DR. BENJAMIN: I am happy to, and my graduates will be happy to help any judicial organization if they are interested to learn more about how to conduct evaluations using really the emergent standards. There are some really good evaluators out there. It was so disheartening to read those words written by that family court evaluator. She was a master's level clinician. Don't get that wrong. A lot of Ph.Ds. will also engage in very sloppy work. What really alarmed me was her refusal to recognize the import of the evidence as she had before her.

PROFESSOR WALLER: If I may jump in with this...?

DR. BENJAMIN: Sure. Please.

PROFESSOR WALLER: One of the things I did not do earlier was give credit to the voice of the court evaluator, Susan DeVries. Did anybody in the room recognize whose voice it was? Wendie Malick of *Just Shoot Me* and *Hot in Cleveland.* The voices that we got, again, all of these people did this for free: Jim Siking, who was Doogie Howser's dad, was one of the FBI agents; Ron Masak was the sheriff on *Murder She Wrote.* John Palmer was an NBC anchor; my ex-husband was one of the judges.

DR. BENJAMIN: You know, the fact they did it for free is significant for psychologists.

PROFESSOR WALLER: That's right, they did it for free. And my ex-boss from NBC was one of the voices; Kathleen Russell of the Center for Judicial Excellence was another voice. But we got all these people to do these voices for free, which was really nice. But when Wendie did it and—you know, those of you who know Wendie, she is a big shot who when she did *Target* she was paid millions of dollars for that. Anyway, I wanted to share that.

DR. BENJAMIN: This is a great segue to my idea. You know, Garland said this in passing, but, boy, Dr. Cummings and Mrs. Cummings, I hope that you heard it, and I hope that you carry away my recommendation that this be pursued with alacrity.

I think we do a terrible job of marketing, the fact that so little has happened despite years of hard work by all of us and by thousands of other people who are concerned about these issues. We have a public relations issue. We need some marketing experts who will take a look at how we can sell what is happening to the American public, because we need people to come out to our state houses and lobby for better funding for victims' rights programs. We need people, victims, as well as professionals, to come out and lobby for changes in the laws regulating the professions that are engaged in the work of this very important process, and that would include jurists, attorneys, and mental health professionals. All of us are regulated under the law, and none of us are performing at the standard of care that we should be performing at. And so we have got a public relations issue here, and, boy, if we all could hire the best public relations folks to get the word out better so that we can have a groundswell of support for making the changes that have to be made. I think that is a terrific idea, Garland.

ATTORNEY KLEINMAN: As I sat with these two days, I actually have a long list of things that I want. You know, I have my wish list. I did not even know we were going to be called upon to do this in this way or I would have brought in my long list.

But I like everything that everybody has asked. But I would like to pick up on one thing that Lenore said off the cuff. It is really a potentially explosive way to deal with some of this, and it takes into account what Andy just said in terms of marketing. And I am not a marketing expert, by any stretch, but we have the wonderful world of the Internet. This is being taped, and I think the idea of a web page, where even if each of these talks are shortened somehow or edited down. I don't know how to do it. I don't know how it can be done, but I think it would be a wonderful way then to provide linkage to other organizations. If we are going to do this across the country and get the word out through the social media, through a Facebook page, through a website, this is one way that it can happen. People could choose what they want and who they want to listen to or read about, and I do not know if it can be done incrementally or if it has to wait until the book is done, but it is something I think that could be tremendously valuable to litigants. And it is not only litigants, the lawyers, the pro se's, the advocates, people who are really doing good work and want to know what is going on out there in other areas in other states. So I think it has a breadth that goes way, way, way beyond what we have done here in the last two days.

JUDGE FIELDS: Toby, if I may, the American Bar Association or any lawyers who are a member of the ABA or if you work not for government, but work as a private practitioner or a legal services lawyer or a lay lawyer, you can join the American Bar Association Domestic Violence Lists, and there are two of them. One is called Litigated and one is called Legislated, and the reason it is separated is that services people cannot be seen to be lobbying, so they are not on the legislated list but they are on the litigated list. And by being on that list, you see national trends. You see the questions that lawyers are raising, urban lawyers, rural lawyers, from every corner of the country, as problems they are encountering in the courts when they represent victims of domestic violence.

Several of the problems that have emerged, like the ones you have been hearing here, or like women being thrown out of public housing or Section 8 housing because they have a violent partner. And that is an issue we dealt with in the 1970s. And I said: Oh, my God. It's come back all over again, like we never dealt with it before.

And there are others like that. So you will see the issues come up. The issue of not having court reporters or tape records or any record being made in the family court is a violation of the constitutional right to due process. You cannot make an appeal. Going on that list might get responses—

JUDGE FIELDS: One of my suggestions for that—and I said to Lenore—was "Talk to the local ACLU. If they won't do it, I would also try Amnesty International." And this is a human rights violation. No question about it. In a court of law, you must have a transcript. And, in fact, we call these courts "courts of re-cord," so where's the record? Traffic court, you have to have a record. Well, if you have to have it in traffic court, this is people's fundamental rights to freedom from violence and for safety. So we have to deal with that question. It must be done. And we need chapter and verse. We need cases—docket numbers. Then you can develop a case with "a record" for an appeal. But the lawyers locally won't do it because they do not want to aggravate the judges before whom they appear regularly. Right. It's just garbage. Do you know what happens when you appeal a judge? You get the judge's respect. They say, "Yes, Ma'am." You walk in, they are your friend. Absolutely. Every time I walked in the family court, my very first year in practice when I was admitted in February of 1971, and by the end of that year, I had seven appeals. Why? Because I was in the New York family court, and the judges deviated from the law that I thought my dog could have probably written the briefs. You walked in. You smelled it. And I walked in to that appellate court and every time I walked in, I got unanimous reversals of the trial court judges. So not only did I make friend in the appellate division, who thought I was just wonderful, but the trial judges in that family court, they didn't mess with me. But I decided my clients deserved better, and we went across the street to the divorce court, because, thank goodness in New York, divorce is not in the family court. It is in the superior. But it was a learning experience for me, but it was also educational for the family court judges. Unfortunately, they have gotten amnesia.

ATTORNEY KLEINMAN: Dr. Cummings, you were standing a moment ago. Did you wish to be recognized, because we welcome it.

DR. CUMMINGS: I appreciate that. This very important dialogue can go for another hour, but unfortunately we have an obligation with the hotel to clear the room at 5:00. So I reluctantly would like to close the proceedings.

Readings

Bancroft, L. & Silverman, J. (2002). *The Batterer as Parent: Addressing the Impact of Domestic Violence on Family Dynamics.* Beverly Hills: Sage.

Benjamin, G.A.H. and Gollan, J.K. (2003). *Family Evaluation in Custody Litigation: Reducing Risks of Ethical Infractions and Malpractice.* Washington, DC: APA Press.

Brave, S.L., Ellman, I.A., & Fabricius, W.V. (2003). Relocation of Children after Divorce and Children's Best Interest: New Evidence and Legal Considerations. *Journal of Family Psychology,* Vol. 17, No. 2, pp. 206-219.

Bodsky, S. (2003). *The Expert Witness.* Washington, DC: APA Press.

Emery, R.E., Otto, R.K., & O'Donohue, W.T. (2005). A Critical Assessment of Child Custody Evaluations: Limited Science and a Flawed System. *Psychological Science in the Public Interest,* Vol. 6, No. 1.pp. 1-29.

Fields, M.D. (2010). Diversion of DV Cases Endangers Victims. *Domestic Violence Report,* Vol. 15, No. 3, pp. 33-48.

Garb, H.N. (2005). Clinical Judgment and Decision Making. *Annual Review of Clinical Psychology,* Vol. 1, No. 1, pp. 67-89.

Hamilton, M.A. (2008). *Justice Denied: What America Must Do to Protect Its Children.* Cambridge, MA: Cambridge University Press.

Hoult, J. (2006). The Evidentiary Admissibility of Parental Alienation Syndrome: Science, Law and Policy. *Children's Legal Rights Journal,* Vol. 26, No. 1, pp. 1-61.

Melton, G., Petrila, J., Poythress, N., & Slobogin C. (2007). *Psychological Evaluations for the Courts: A Handbook for Mental Health Professionals and Lawyers* (3rd Edition). New York: Guilford.

Newberger, E.H. (2000). *The Men They Will Become.* Cambridge, MA: Da Capo Press.

Schafran, L.H. (1994). Gender Bias in Family Courts. *Family Advocate,* Vol. 17, No. 1, pp. 22-28.

Sullivan, I. (2010). *Raised by the Courts.* New York: Kaplan.

Walker, L.E. (Ed.) (1984). *Women and Mental Health Policy.* Beverly Hills, CA: Sage.